William Shakespeare

VIP

Very Interesting People

Peter Holland

OXFORD
UNIVERSITY PRESS

OXFORD
UNIVERSITY PRESS

Great Clarendon Street, Oxford ox2 6DP

Oxford University Press is a department of the University of Oxford.
It furthers the University's objective of excellence in research, scholarship,
and education by publishing worldwide in

Oxford New York

Auckland Cape Town Dar es Salaam Hong Kong Karachi
Kuala Lumpur Madrid Melbourne Mexico City Nairobi
New Delhi Shanghai Taipei Toronto

With offices in

Argentina Austria Brazil Chile Czech Republic France Greece
Guatemala Hungary Italy Japan Poland Portugal Singapore
South Korea Switzerland Thailand Turkey Ukraine Vietnam

Oxford is a registered trade mark of Oxford University Press
in the UK and in certain other countries

Published in the United States
by Oxford University Press Inc., New York

First published in the *Oxford Dictionary of National Biography* 2004
This paperback edition first published 2007

First published 2007

British Library Cataloguing in Publication Data

Data available

Library of Congress Cataloging in Publication Data

Data available

Typeset by SPI Publisher Services, Pondicherry, India
Printed in Great Britain
on acid-free paper by
Clays Ltd, St Ives plc

ISBN 978–0–19–921283–5 (Pbk.)

10 9 8 7 6 5 4 3 2

Contents

Preface

In July 1897, volume 51 of the original *Dictionary of National Biography* was published, containing, in this instalment, the life of Shakespeare written by Sidney Lee who was by then editor of the *DNB* and would, by the end of the project, be the author of more than 800 entries. When, almost exactly a century later, I received a letter inviting me to write the biography of Shakespeare for the new *Oxford Dictionary of National Biography*, I was the author of one entry: for an eighteenth-century actor so obscure that I had barely heard of him. Lee republished his biography in 1898 as *A Life of William Shakespeare*, greatly extending the article to at first over 450 pages and, in later revisions, nearly 800. This book reprints my piece exactly as it appears in the latest on-line version of the *Oxford DNB*. One characteristic, though, is shared by Lee's article and my own: in both cases the entry on Shakespeare was one of the longest in the whole multi-volumed work, a sign of Shakespeare's preeminence as England's national poet.

Writing the biography, weighing the evidence afresh, and finding the right concise formulation for all the imponderables and doubts was hard work. But what most attracted me to the project—and what makes this short biography of Shakespeare unlike most others much longer—was the insistence of Colin Matthew, the *Oxford DNB*'s first editor and prime mover, that the details of Shakespeare's life would take up less than half the entry and that the rest would trace Shakespeare's after-lives, the many ways in which his works have been performed, rewritten, and translated, and have influenced writers, thinkers, audiences, school-children, students, poets, painters, composers, and choreographers across the world. In financial terms, Shakespeare is Britain's most successful export; in cultural terms, his plays have profoundly informed cultures across the world.

I am writing this preface a few days after returning from the World Shakespeare Congress in Brisbane, a sign of the global health of the academic Shakespeare industry, and before leaving for Stratford-upon-Avon to sample some productions in the Royal Shakespeare Company's 'The Complete Works' season (advertised as 'The greatest dramatist, the essential year'), which, judging from the ticket-sales, is a sign of the health of Shakespeare on stage. Important new biographies of Shakespeare have appeared every year since I wrote the article (in 2001–2) and the best—or most hyped—appear in the bestseller lists; editions of the plays and poems are the backbone of many publishers' lists and of their profits; new films of his plays, often in strange disguises, are released each year, for instance *She's the Man*, a version of *Twelfth Night*, that I watched on the plane back from Australia; and new alternative candidates for the authorship of the plays are advanced with similar regularity (Sir Henry Neville and Mary Herbert, countess of Pembroke, being the latest to join the band). However one looks at it, 'Shakespeare' is alive and well and this brief biography of his life and afterlives will, I hope, give its readers some sense of that remarkable history.

Peter Holland
August 2006

About the author

Peter Holland is McMeel Family Professor in Shakespeare Studies in the Department of Film, Television, and Theatre at the University of Notre Dame, Indiana. He is editor of *Shakespeare Survey* and co-General Editor of *Oxford Shakespeare Topics* (with Stanley Wells) and *Great Shakespeareans* (with Adrian Poole).

1

Background, early life, and marriage

William Shakespeare (1564–1616), playwright and poet, was baptized, probably by the parish priest, John Bretchgirdle, in Holy Trinity, the parish church of Stratford upon Avon, on 26 April 1564, the third child of John Shakespeare (*d.* 1601) and Mary Arden (*d.* 1608). It seems appropriate that the first of many gaps in the records of Shakespeare's life should be the exact date of his birth, though that is a common problem for the period. He was probably born on 21, 22, or 23 April 1564, given the 1559 prayer book's instructions to parents on the subject of baptisms. But, ever since Joseph Greene, an eighteenth-century Stratford curate, informed the scholar George Steevens that Shakespeare was born on 23 April, with no apparent evidence for his assertion, and Steevens adopted that date in his 1773 edition of Shakespeare, it has been usual to assume that Shakespeare was born on St George's day, so that England's patron saint and the birth of the 'national poet' can be celebrated on the same day. Where he was born is clearer: in 1564 his parents appear to have been living in Henley Street, probably in part of the building now known as Shakespeare's Birthplace but, equally probably, not in that part of the building in which the room traditionally known as the place of Shakespeare's birth is located. The accretion of myth and commerce around Shakespeare's biography and its material legacy produces such paradoxes.

Shakespeare's family

Richard Shakespeare, a husbandman and probably John's father, had settled in Snitterfield near Stratford by 1529 and had died by February 1561, leaving property that he rented from Robert Arden of Wilmcote. Robert Arden was a member of the younger branch of the powerful Arden family; his father, Thomas Arden, lived at Wilmcote and passed lands, probably quite extensive, to his son. Robert married twice: with his first wife, Agnes Hill, *née* Webbe, he had at least eight children, all girls, the youngest of whom was Mary; there appear to have been no children from the second marriage, though there were stepchildren.

The two families, Ardens and Shakespeares, were linked by Richard Shakespeare's tenancy from Robert Arden. But John Shakespeare (*b.*in or before 1530, *d.* 1601) did not continue his father's occupation. By the time he married Mary Arden (some time between November 1556 and 1558), he had established himself in Stratford as a glover and whittawer (a dresser of light-coloured leather). He lived in Henley Street, buying a house and garden there in 1556 and starting to buy further property in town. In this he might well have been helped by his wife's inheritance: in Robert Arden's will of November 1556 she was named one of the two executors and supervised the substantial inventory of his goods and moveables in December 1556 after his death. She also inherited the valuable estate in

Wilmcote known as Asbies, land that on her marriage came to her husband.

John and Mary Shakespeare were probably married in Aston Cantlow, the parish church for Wilmcote and the place where Robert Arden wanted to be buried. The exact date of the wedding is unknown but their first child, Joan, was born in September 1558 (and may well have died in infancy); Margaret was baptized in December 1562 and was buried the following April. A year later William was born. He survived the devastating plague that killed one in eight of the town's population later the same year. There were five more children: Gilbert (1566–1612), another Joan (born 1569, indicating that John and Mary's first child must have died by that year; she was the only sibling to outlive William, dying in 1646), Anne (1571–1579), Richard (1574–1613), and Edmund (1580–1607). All but Anne lived to adulthood. William's childhood was thus spent in a steadily increasing family and there were other relatives nearby: his uncle Henry Shakespeare, John's brother, lived in Snitterfield and many of his mother's sisters married local men.

John Shakespeare bought more property in Stratford in 1575, almost certainly including the rest of the 'Birthplace', creating a substantial house which even though it incorporated space for his workshop amounted to a fine home for his expanding family. But this period was also one of ever-increasing civic importance for John Shakespeare. He had risen through the lesser offices of the borough and, by the time of William's birth, was one of the fourteen burgesses of Stratford. In 1565 he became an alderman and in 1568 was elected bailiff for the year, the highest office in the town. In 1571 he became chief alderman and deputy bailiff. At about this time he also seems to have applied for a coat of arms. The family's wealth was also growing and the civic importance and high social standing that John Shakespeare had achieved in a brief period provided the context for William's upbringing.

But in the following years something seems to have gone wrong with John Shakespeare's finances. At the start of the 1570s he was stretching his commercial activities beyond his trade, dealing illegally in wool and also being prosecuted for usury. By the end of the decade he was in debt; in 1578 he mortgaged some of Mary's inheritance and lost it in 1580 when he could not repay the sum, land that would otherwise have been inherited by William in due course. He stopped attending council meetings after 1576 as well, and was replaced as an alderman in 1586. All of this too provided a family context for William's youth; the decline in John Shakespeare's fortunes cannot have been unaccompanied by anxiety.

In 1592 John was listed by the presenters for the parish of Stratford upon Avon as an obstinate recusant, among nine on the list whose absence was identified by the presenters and by the commissioners to whom they reported as being 'for feare of processe for Debtte' (Schoenbaum, *Documentary Life*, 39). There is no self-evident reason to distrust this statement, though it has been seen as an excuse to cover secret Catholicism. Certainly some Catholics feigned debt as a reason for recusancy but John Shakespeare's debts seem real enough.

In 1790 a bricklayer was reported as having found in 1757 in the roof of the Henley Street house a manuscript now known as John Shakespeare's spiritual testament. Blank copies of this formulaic document, based on one written by Cardinal Borromeo, are claimed to have been circulated in large numbers by Catholic missionaries; this copy was said to have been completed by or on behalf of John Shakespeare. Transcribed by the great Shakespeare scholar Edmond Malone, who later came to doubt its authenticity, it is now lost and its link to John Jordan, a Stratford man well known for inventing materials to satisfy the increasing thirst for Shakespeariana, puts it under suspicion. In the unlikely event that it was genuine it would suggest that John Shakespeare was a Catholic still holding to his original faith and that William was brought up in a household where the double standards of adequate outward observance of protestant orthodoxy and private heterodoxy were largely achieved. There is, of course, no reason to assume that the adult William shared his father's religious views, and the evidence for John's being a Catholic is very far from decisive. It was, after all, during John Shakespeare's time as bailiff in 1568 that the images of the last judgment that decorated the guild chapel in Stratford were whitewashed and defaced as no longer acceptable to state protestantism, though this might simply have been a further example of John's outward conformism.

Shakespeare's education

In any case, another event during John Shakespeare's tenure as bailiff seems more significant for his son's future career: the visit to Stratford of two theatre companies, the Queen's Players and Worcester's Men, the first time theatre companies are known to have played in Stratford. Since the first performance in any town was usually in front of the town officials, John Shakespeare would have seen the performances and William might well have accompanied him (as other children certainly did in similar circumstances). Further visits followed: Leicester's Men in 1572 and 1576, Warwick's Men in 1574, Worcester's Men in 1574 and 1581, Lord Strange's Men in 1578, Essex's Men in 1578 and 1583, Derby's Men in 1579,

Lord Berkeley's Men in 1580 and 1582. Across the period when William was likely to have been continuously resident in Stratford, there were at least thirteen visits by companies of players, bringing a fairly wide repertory of drama, little of which can be confidently identified. None the less, there is a context there for William Shakespeare's early learning about theatre performance and contemporary drama in the work of such professional companies. He might, too, have travelled nearby to see the spectacular entertainments at Kenilworth given by the earl of Leicester for the queen in 1575, or the magnificent cycle drama of mystery plays which was still performed annually at Coventry until 1578, or Coventry's Hocktide play (suppressed in 1568 but performed again at Kenilworth in 1575), or the amateur performances which regularly occurred in Stratford.

Shakespeare would also have acted, as part of his education, either in Latin plays or in oratorical declamation, the latter a crucial part of the performative training in classical rhetoric. William's own education was not likely to have been affected by his father's fluctuating fortunes. It was also probably far better than either of his parents had received. There is no evidence that either John or Mary Shakespeare could write: each signed with a kind of mark. But the marks were not the awkward crosses of the totally illiterate: John often drew a fine pair of compasses; Mary's mark in 1579 was a complex design, apparently incorporating her initials and fluently written. Both may well have been able to read: many who could not write could read. Certainly, given John's status in the community, his four sons would have gone to Stratford's grammar school where their education would have been free. Before that William would have attended 'petty school' from about the age of five to about seven, learning to read.

At the King's New School, Stratford's splendid grammar school, William would have learned an immense amount of Latin literature and history, perhaps using the Latin–English dictionary left to the school by John Bretchgirdle who had baptized him. Among the works that Shakespeare later used as sources for his plays are a number that he would have read as part of his grammar-school education: the history of Livy, the speeches of Cicero, the comedies of Plautus and Terence, the tragedies of Seneca, and the poetry of Virgil and, above all, Ovid, who remained his favourite poet. The range of Latin writing that formed the curriculum was, by modern standards, vast. The mode of teaching, by a good teacher assisted by an usher, was one calculated to ensure the arts of memory, facility in composition, and rhetorical skills.

In addition, regular attendance at church, a legal requirement which his father does not appear to have avoided until later, guaranteed prolonged exposure to the Book of Homilies (fairly dull), the Book of Common Prayer (rather more exciting), and, especially, the exhilarating language of the Bible in English, a resource that Shakespeare, like his contemporaries, knew well, used extensively, and embedded deeply into the fabric of his language.

After school, and marriage: the 'lost years'

Leaving school at about fifteen, Shakespeare would have had a series of options open. He might have gone into his father's trade as an apprentice and there is anecdotal evidence to that effect recorded by John Aubrey in the late seventeenth century, also noting that 'when he kill'd a Calfe, he would doe it in a *high style*, & make a Speech' (Schoenbaum, *Documentary Life*, 58), though, since John Shakespeare's trade did not involve

8 slaughtering, this could possibly refer to William's acting in a mumming play or Whitsun 'pastime' of the kind the town council paid for in 1583—pretending to kill a calf was a trick often included in such plays.

John Aubrey's conversation with William Beeston, son of Christopher who had worked with Shakespeare later in the Lord Chamberlain's Men, produced the snippet of information that Shakespeare 'had been in his younger yeares a Schoolmaster in the Countrey' (Schoenbaum, *Documentary Life*, 59). The theory is not impossible and has gained ground in the wake of the re-examination of the evidence surrounding the mention in 1581 of a 'William Shakeshafte' in the will of Alexander de Hoghton of Lea Hall in Lancashire, encouraging Sir Thomas Hesketh to take on Shakeshaft as a servant. Shakeshaft was a common name in Lancashire, not least in the area surrounding the Hoghton family estates, and an extremely uncommon one in Warwickshire; none of the many variant spellings of William Shakespeare's own name even begins to approximate to Shakeshaft.

John Cottom, who was the teacher at Stratford grammar school from 1579 to 1581 and hence during or just after Shakespeare's last year at school, then returned to his family in Lancashire; his younger brother was a Catholic priest who was tried with Edmund Campion and executed in 1582. Perhaps, the theory runs, Cottom encouraged Shakespeare, as a member of a recusant Catholic family, to be a schoolteacher in a staunchly Catholic household in the north of England. The evidence is purely circumstantial and the crucial evidence, the mention of William Shakeshaft, is insufficient for proof. In any case, Shakespeare was rather less qualified to be a schoolmaster than any of the Stratford teachers he had studied under.

One advantage of the theory is that it suggests a route for Shakespeare to move to London since there were links between Hesketh and Hoghton and Ferdinando Stanley, Lord Strange (later earl of Derby), whose company of players might well have included Shakespeare but was more certainly the troupe that acted a number of Shakespeare's early plays.

But there is no reason to posit a direct link for Shakespeare between Lancashire and London, if he was ever in Lancashire at all, since by 1582 he was certainly back in Stratford. On 27 November a marriage licence was issued for Shakespeare's marriage to Anne Hathaway (1555/6–1623) (though the record in the bishop of Worcester's register mistakenly refers to the bride as Anne Whateley of Temple Grafton) and on the following day a bond was issued binding Fulke Sandells and John Richardson for the sum of £40 as surety for the marriage, a necessary step since William was at eighteen still a minor and needed his father's consent to the match. Sandells and Richardson had both in 1581 been named in the will of Richard Hathaway, Anne's father, a yeoman farmer of Shottery, a village just outside Stratford; the will left Anne 10 marks, to be paid when she married.

Anne (whose name also appears as Agnes) was the eldest of Richard's seven children (three with his first wife and four with his second); William may have been a minor, distinctly young for marriage at this time, but Anne was of a normal marrying age. The Shakespeares and Hathaways knew each other: John Shakespeare had acted as surety for Richard Hathaway and twice paid his debts. Whatever the nature of William's relationship with Anne may have been—and biographers and novelists have frequently speculated about it—by the end of summer 1582 Anne was pregnant and the marriage in November was performed after only a single reading of the banns, rather than the more normal three, presumably in order to speed up the process. The vicar who officiated at Temple Grafton, if that was indeed where they married, was John Frith, known for his ability to cure hawks but also 'Unsound in religion', according to a survey in 1586 of the Warwickshire clergy, again a possible indication of Shakespeare's Catholicism (Schoenbaum, *Documentary Life*, 71).

It is reasonable to give in to temptation and assign Shakespeare's Sonnet 145 to this period, making it Shakespeare's earliest extant work: its final couplet puns on Hathaway (' "I hate" from hate away she threw,/And saved my life, saying "not you." ' Sonnet 145, ll. 13–14) and its octosyllabics, unusual in the sonnets, suggest that it may not have been part of the sequence originally. There is no especial reason why a man should write a love poem to a woman only at the beginning of their relationship and the poem need not relate to any actual moment in the history of William and Anne. But, if it were written at the time of the event it appears to describe, then its description of courtship rather than marriage would date it to the early 1580s.

Six months after the marriage, on 26 May 1583, Susanna Shakespeare was baptized, followed on 2 February 1585 by William's and Anne's twins, Hamnet and Judith, probably named after Hamnet and Judith Sadler. Hamnet Sadler, a local baker, was in 1616 one of the witnesses of Shakespeare's will, and his name also appears in local records as Hamlet. With these three children Shakespeare's family seems to have been complete: there are no records of further children. Some have used this as evidence that the marriage was distant or unhappy, though many happily married couples both then and later have had no children at all and it is perhaps relevant that Susanna and Judith had few children (one and three respectively).

From 1585 to 1592 the records of Shakespeare's life are almost silent. He is briefly referred to in records concerning the attempts of his parents to retrieve property in Wilmcote, part of what had been Mary's inheritance and should have been passed on to William, land that had been mortgaged and was now lost, another indication of John's financial troubles. But the reference does not indicate his presence in Stratford. Biographers have created fanciful narratives for this period; none have any foundation. Perhaps this was when he was 'a Schoolmaster in the Countrey'. The traditional explanation, first set out by Nicholas Rowe in his biographical sketch prefixed to his 1709 edition of Shakespeare's plays, was that William poached deer from Sir Thomas Lucy's estate at Charlecote, was caught and prosecuted, wrote a ballad against Lucy, and was forced to escape to London to avoid further prosecution. Shakespeare's apparent jibe at the Lucy coat of arms in *The Merry Wives of Windsor* (I.i, ll. 13–20) has been explained as belated revenge, though why Shakespeare waited so long and revenged himself so obscurely is not adequately justified.

Making a career: early plays and poems

2

Shakespeare the player

The next print reference to Shakespeare is in *Greenes Groats-Worth of Witte* (1592), a pamphlet ostensibly by Robert Greene (though possibly written by someone else, probably Henry Chettle) and published after Greene's death in September 1592; the pamphlet attacks Shakespeare as:

> an upstart Crow, beautified with our feathers, that with his *Tygers hart wrapt in a Players hyde*, supposes he is as well able to bombast out a blanke verse as the best of you: and beeing an absolute *Iohannes fac totum*, is in his owne conceit the onely Shake-scene in a countrey. (*Greenes Groats-Worth of Witte*, 1592, sig. F1*r*)

The passage transforms the Duke of York's vicious attack on the even more vicious Queen Margaret in *3 Henry VI*: 'O tiger's heart wrapped in a woman's hide!' (I.iv, l. 138).

Whatever else Shakespeare may have been doing between 1585 and 1592 it is clear that he had been and was still an actor, that he had now become a playwright, and that, whatever other jobs this jack of all trades ('Iohannes fac totum') was doing in the theatre, he had become well enough known to irritate Robert Greene or whoever wrote the pamphlet. The attack was so sharp that Henry Chettle, who had been responsible for its publication, is often thought to be apologizing to Shakespeare later that year in his *Kind-Hartes Dreame* for not having 'moderated the heate' in preparing the piece for the press, praising Shakespeare for as 'divers of worship have reported, his uprightnes of dealing, which argues his honesty, and his fa[ce]tious grace in writting, which aprooves his Art' (H. Chettle, *Kind-Hartes Dreame*, 1592, sigs. A3*v*–4*r*), though the passage is probably an apology to someone other than Shakespeare.

Neither at this period nor later is there any firm evidence of the roles Shakespeare acted or of the quality of his performances. Anecdotes ascribe to him various roles in his own plays, for example Adam in *As You Like It*, a choice which does not suggest any especially great thespian talent. He is named first in the list of 'the Principall Actors in all these Playes' in the collection of his own works in 1623 and appears in the lists of actors in Ben Jonson's *Workes* (1616) for *Every Man in his Humour* ('first Acted, in the yeere 1598') and *Sejanus his Fall* (1603). However much or little he may have acted, it is significant that he was known as a player, for example in the sneer by Ralph Brooke, the York herald, in 1602 at the grant of arms to 'Shakespear the Player' (Schoenbaum, *Documentary Life*, 172).

When Shakespeare became a player is not clear but it is at least possible that he joined the Queen's Men. They played in Stratford in 1587 and their repertory included a play based on Montemayor's *Diana* (the source for Shakespeare's *The Two Gentlemen of Verona*), anonymous plays on the reigns of King John (*The Troublesome Reign*), Richard III (*The True Tragedy*),

Henry IV, and Henry V (both covered by *The Famous Victories of Henry V*), all subjects of plays by Shakespeare himself in the 1590s, as well as *King Leir* which, as well as being the major source for Shakespeare's *King Lear*, has possibly left its trace on a number of his earlier works. Though he was influenced by many other plays, not least the work of Christopher Marlowe, in developing his own style in his early works, there is no comparable body of sustained influence. If not actually in the Queen's Men, he certainly seems to have known their work especially well and the plays that belonged to them were crucial to Shakespeare's histories, the works that established the Lord Chamberlain's Men as the pre-eminent company of the age. The Queen's Men's works were virulently anti-Catholic and the company may even have owed its existence to a political aim of touring anti-Catholic propaganda; Shakespeare's plays that owe something of their existence to the Queen's Men's repertory, while hardly being Catholic apologetics, are strikingly less factional in their religion. The idea that Shakespeare joined the company in 1587 after one of their actors, William Knell, died in a fight in Thame, Oxfordshire, is no more improbable than the deer-poaching narrative.

First plays: *Henry VI*

Determining what Shakespeare had done to warrant the attack in *Greenes Groats-Worth of Witte* is exceptionally difficult. The dating of Shakespeare's works is often opaque and the early plays pose especial problems. Some scholars argue for the plays to have been written both earlier and in a radically different order from the conventionally accepted sequence. Each reordering produces a new narrative for Shakespeare's contact with other plays and other dramatists, his reading, and his development as a dramatist. While there is uncertainty for the dating of the early plays there is equal uncertainty over authorship. Collaboration was common for playwrights generating drama at high speed to satisfy the appetite of the theatre companies and their customers. The evidence of Philip Henslowe's accounts shows that a minority of plays had a single author, at least for the repertory performed by the companies to which these records relate. If arguments for collaboration in plays in the Shakespeare canon are no longer based solely on a notion of quality (that which is good is by Shakespeare, that which is bad is by a collaborator), the evidence derived from analysis of the plays themselves—their technique, staging, use of rhyme, rare words, common words, feminine endings in blank verse, and other tests—is not susceptible to final verification.

By the time Shakespeare was attacked for his arrogance in being a playwright in 1592, he had certainly written *3 Henry VI*. The other two parts of his exploration of the reign of Henry VI had also been performed. *Part 2*, originally published in 1594 as *The First Part of the Contention betwixt the Two Famous Houses of York and Lancaster*, may have been the first to be performed. It is likely that *Part 3*, published in 1595 as *The True Tragedy of Richard Duke of York*, was next to be written and performed and that *Part 1* was the new play called 'Harey the vj' that Henslowe recorded as performed by Lord Strange's Men at the Rose Theatre on 3 March 1592.

The decision to write plays on English history was a response to the current popularity of such drama. The idea of a two-part play was probably a response to the phenomenal success of Marlowe's *Tamburlaine*, though there were many other two-part plays. There are strong indications, not least in the title by which *2 Henry VI* was first known, that Shakespeare had mapped out the drama as at least a two-part exploration of a catastrophic period of English history. But his decision to create a three-part work was an innovation. Shakespeare's first investigation of English history generated a work on a scale that had no dramatic precedent in the professional theatre. Its nearest analogy was the biblical cycle-drama, the 'mystery' plays which were still being performed in his boyhood. But the move from sacred to secular also produced a form of theatrical analogue to the chronicle histories, the massive prose narratives out of which Shakespeare constructed his plays, particularly Edward Halle's *The Union of the Two Noble and Illustre Families of Lancaster and York* (1548) and Raphael Holinshed's *The Chronicles of England, Scotland, and Ireland* of which Shakespeare used the second edition of 1587. He read other chronicles as well, implying the availability to him of a substantial library, and these plays show the first small traces of his use of works that he would return to for local and general inspiration throughout his career: Apuleius's *The Golden Ass* in Adlington's 1566 translation and Ovid's *Metamorphoses* in Arthur Golding's version completed in 1567.

1 Henry VI in particular was an immediate success. In 1592 Thomas Nashe wondered in *Pierce Penilesse*:

> How would it have joyed brave *Talbot* (the terror of the French) to thinke … hee should triumphe againe on the Stage, and have his bones newe embalmed with the teares of ten thousand spectators at least, (at severall times) who, in the Tragedian that represents his person, imagine they behold him fresh bleeding. (Schoenbaum, *Documentary Life*, 120)

Nashe's praise might be exaggerated, not least by the likelihood that he co-wrote *Part 1*. It looks as though Shakespeare himself wrote only a comparatively small part of *Part 1* and that Nashe and at least two other dramatists had their hands in it. But the three plays that make up *Henry VI* established Shakespeare as a powerful and popular dramatist.

Early comedies, *Titus Andronicus*, *Richard III*, and 'Sir Thomas More'

It is likely that Greene (or whoever wrote the pamphlet) could also have been responding to Shakespeare's first comedies, for *The Two Gentlemen of Verona* and *The Taming of the Shrew* were probably also written at this time. The theatres were closed because of the plague for almost the whole period between June 1592 and June 1594, interrupting Shakespeare's career as a playwright, except for the appearance of *Titus Andronicus*, probably first performed at the Rose Theatre on 24 January 1594. *Titus*, Shakespeare's first tragedy, shows further influences: Ovid's *Metamorphoses* as a profoundly determining source for plots, speeches, language, and emotional power; Seneca's tragedies, filtered now through translations and popular adaptations; and, above all, the need to work through and resolve for himself the challenge presented by the theatrical power achieved by his greatest contemporary, Marlowe. *Titus* also shows Shakespeare working with another collaborator, for George Peele was probably responsible for act I of the play. *Titus Andronicus* was immediately, and remained, popular, also attested by the survival of a drawing by Henry Peacham of a scene derived from the play and by a performance for Sir John Harington at Burley on the Hill in 1596.

The effective closure of the theatres may have also delayed the first performance of *Richard III*. It seems likely that Shakespeare wrote the play not too long after finishing the *Henry VI* trilogy, extending its scope and taking the narrative up to the accession of Henry VII and the inauguration of the Tudor dynasty. But the culminating part is radically different from its predecessors in its exploration of character with its astonishing creation of Richard as comic villain and, in the speech Richard is given on waking after the nightmare appearance of the ghosts of his victims on the night before the battle of Bosworth, with the discovery of a dramatic language never heard before in English drama in its depiction of the inner workings of a disordered mind. It is as if at this moment Shakespeare unlocks the vast potential of dramatic character and of the blank verse form for the first time. Perhaps this may have been a consequence of the delay caused by the plague.

Something of Shakespeare's growing status perhaps at this time is indicated by his participation in the writing of 'Sir Thomas More'. The play, never printed, survives in a manuscript written by a number of hands. It is likely, though not absolutely certain, that Hand D, as it is known, is Shakespeare's and that this is therefore the only piece of his writing other than signatures to survive. The play was first written by Anthony Munday, perhaps with help from Henry Chettle, in 1592 or 1593. At some point thereafter, possibly in 1593 or 1594 (though equally possibly, as some have argued, as late as 1600–04), the play was heavily revised with, among others, Shakespeare (that is, Hand D) being called in to rewrite the scene where More stops the May day riots directed against immigrants in London. Collaborative writing in the period often divided plays up according to different writers' specialisms and Hand D, as a kind of play-doctor, was plainly recognized both as especially proficient in the writing of crowd scenes (as the Jack Cade scenes in *2 Henry VI* had demonstrated) and as someone of proven worth who could effectively resolve the difficulties. Ironically, Sir Edmund Tilney, master of the revels, approved the play provided that the scenes of the 'insurrection' were left out, though this may well refer to the scenes before Shakespeare revised them.

The manuscript itself reveals much about Shakespeare's mode of composition and linguistic preferences with widely varying spellings. Jonson commented (in *Timber*, first printed in 1641), 'the Players have often mentioned it as an honour to *Shakespeare*, that in his writing, (whatsoever he penn'd) hee never blotted out line My answer hath beene, Would he had blotted a thousand' (Vickers, 1.26). But, though the passages by Hand D are far cleaner than many rough drafts, Hand D often changed his mind, blotting and interlineating as he went, often, it would appear, leaving out speech-prefixes of individual members of the crowd (and often marking them simply as 'other' or 'all') as if the dialogue had to be written without the names of speakers really mattering. The sheets in Hand D are as close as we are ever likely to come to Shakespeare in the throes of composition.

About the same date, possibly in 1592 or 1593, Shakespeare contributed a sequence to another play. The main author or authors of *King Edward III* (published in 1596) are unknown but Shakespeare wrote the episode of the king's unsuccessful wooing of the Countess of Salisbury, a witty and moving passage, markedly better than the rest of a mundane play and another indication of Shakespeare's recognition by his fellow dramatists as a writer well worth employing to improve a play.

Narrative poems

While the theatre companies toured the provinces and waited for the plague to abate far enough to enable the theatres to be permitted to reopen, Shakespeare turned to another kind of writing, Ovidian narrative poetry. *Venus and Adonis* was published in 1593, printed by Richard Field (*b*. 1561), who had also come to London from Stratford upon Avon and may well have been Shakespeare's friend in childhood. Field had been apprenticed to Thomas Vautrollier, before taking over the business in 1590; Vautrollier had printed in 1579 Sir Thomas North's translation from Plutarch, *The Lives of the Noble Grecians and Romans*, and Field printed a revised edition in 1595, a volume that Shakespeare used extensively in play after play. Perhaps he bought books from Field or, just as likely, borrowed them from his fellow Stratfordian.

The publication of *Venus and Adonis* in 1593, the first printing of any work by Shakespeare, is perhaps less significant than the poem's dedication, signed by Shakespeare to mark his authorship and offering 'the first heir of my invention' to Henry Wriothesley, third earl of Southampton. A brilliant mixture of comedy and eroticism, *Venus and Adonis* was Shakespeare's most popular work, if the number of reprints is a guide, with at least fifteen editions by 1636. If the tone of this dedication is formal, the language of the dedication to *The Rape of Lucrece*, printed by Field in 1594, speaks of a far closer friendship: 'What I have done is yours; what I have to do is yours, being part in all I have, devoted yours.' In the dedication to *Venus and Adonis*, he vowed to 'take advantage of all idle hours till I have honoured you with some graver labour'; *Lucrece*, with its violently erotic account of rape, passionate description of suicide, and serious portrayal of the overthrow of monarchy, is the powerful outcome of that promise. Both poems were widely alluded to and equally widely praised, apparently the first works by Shakespeare to gain wide approval from young, educated, fashionable male readers; as Gabriel Harvey noted, probably in 1601, 'The younger sort takes much delight in

Shakespeares Venus, & Adonis: but his Lucrece, & his tragedie of Hamlet, Prince of Denmarke, have it in them, to please the wiser sort' (Chambers, 2.197).

Shakespeare's toying in *Venus and Adonis* with a desire for the male body that is as much homoerotic as heterosexual might well have endeared the poem to Southampton. Rowe's account in 1709 that Southampton gave Shakespeare the vast sum of £1000 is not credible; however, it might have been exaggerated from a smaller gift. But Rowe describes it as enabling Shakespeare 'to go through with a Purchase which he heard he had a mind to' (*Works*, ed. Rowe, 1.x). There were three possible major pieces of expenditure to which this might relate: the acquisition of a share in the theatre company, the granting of a coat of arms, and the purchase of New Place, all three of which will be considered below. That the poems gained Shakespeare both money and a powerful friend, rather than simply the formal approval of an aristocratic patron, seems likely. A cryptic poem, *Willobie his Avisa* (published in 1594), may, in its comments on H. W. and W. S., allude to a friendship or even a love affair between Southampton and Shakespeare.

The Lord Chamberlain's Men

Before the plague most of Shakespeare's plays were probably written for and sold to Lord Strange's Men, later the Earl of Derby's Men, though *2* and *3 Henry VI* and possibly *The Taming of the Shrew* were performed by Pembroke's Men, a company which flourished briefly in London between 1591 and 1593. If one notes the prominence of Lord Stanley, the Earl of Derby, in *Richard III*, then it may be a careful compliment to the current earl of Derby as the players' patron; if one sees the character as a perfect time-server who does his best to stay out of the battle until he can align himself with the winning side, then it may be rather less of a compliment. *Richard III* may be the last play Shakespeare wrote with Strange's Men in mind.

The effect of plague and the difficulty of making a profit by touring affected all the playing companies. The history of the theatre companies in London, their repertory and resources in this period, is as murky as much else to do with Shakespeare's life. *Titus Andronicus*, for instance, was performed by the three different companies named on the title-page of its first printing in 1594: Derby's (that is, Lord Strange's Men), Pembroke's, and Sussex's players; but it could have been either by each successively or by a company containing members of all three. But in May 1594 Henry Carey, Lord Hunsdon, who was lord chamberlain, and his son-in-law Charles, Lord Howard, the lord admiral and previous lord chamberlain, created something approaching a duopoly for their players in London. After the companies had briefly played as a combined company at Newington Butts in June 1594 (including performances of *Titus Andronicus*), the abatement of the plague meant that they could properly return to the city. The Lord Admiral's Men took up residence at the Rose Theatre. Hunsdon's Men, now known as the Lord Chamberlain's Men, including some of the best actors of Derby's and Pembroke's companies, played at The Theatre to the north-east of the city, beginning their long and unequalled period as the greatest company of actors in the country.

From this point on all Shakespeare's new plays were written for and belonged to the Lord Chamberlain's Men. What is more, payments to the company for their court performances over the Christmas season of 1594 name Shakespeare with William Kemp, the company's clown, and Richard Burbage, their leading actor, as the three payees, indicating their pre-eminent status among the small group of sharers in the company. Though often called actor-sharers, the participants in the Chamberlain's Men were unlikely to have included Shakespeare on the grounds of his acting ability. Uniquely among playwrights of the period, Shakespeare began a long and uninterrupted association with and participation in one particular theatre company, rather than, as it were, accepting freelance work for whoever would pay. Though later dramatists like John Fletcher, Philip Massinger, Richard Brome, and James Shirley had similar links to a particular company—in Brome's case explicitly set out in a contract—none seem to have been sharers. Shakespeare was not only the Chamberlain's Men's house dramatist, producing on average two plays a year for them until his retirement, but also a close participant in their developing business.

Either on the grounds of his reputation as a playwright alone or by virtue of a payment, Shakespeare had acquired a share in the new company and received his share of their fluctuating but sizeable profits over the rest of his life. The share also altered as the number of sharers varied, going from one-tenth in 1599 up to one-eighth when Will Kemp left and down to a twelfth and a fourteenth as further sharers were brought in. If the share was bought it was a shrewd investment, giving Shakespeare a certain amount of security of income, but it also conferred status on him as, in effect, a partner in a profit-sharing collective enterprise.

Fame in London, prosperity in Stratford

3

Plays, 1594–1598

In December 1594 the Chamberlain's Men performed *The Comedy of Errors* at Gray's Inn. The play's design as a classical farce based on Plautus's *Menaechmi*, a play Shakespeare might well have read at school, made it especially suitable for the Christmas revels of the young gentry at one of the inns of court. In the course of the next year or so the company also performed *Love's Labour's Lost*, probably its lost sequel 'Love's Labour's Won', *Richard II*, *Romeo and Juliet*, and *A Midsummer Night's Dream*, an extraordinary output that was perhaps the result of Shakespeare's busy writing activity during the plague time. In the flow of creativity in this period and with the imprecision inevitable in attempting to date the plays' writing and first performances accurately, other work may also belong to this period or even earlier: *King John* was probably written in 1595 or 1596, a history play which, like *Richard II*, was written without being part of a sequence and which, in its extraordinary veering of tone from fully blown tragedy to mocking and satiric comedy, marks Shakespeare's most extreme view of the action of history and the legitimacy of kingship.

Shakespeare's plays were also now beginning to be printed: unauthorized versions of *2* and *3 Henry VI* appeared in 1594 and 1595 respectively; *Titus Andronicus* was published in 1594. A version of *The Taming of the Shrew*, with different character names and considerable adjustment of the plot, also appeared in 1594 as *The Taming of a Shrew*. Some of this print activity may have been the result of the collapse of the companies which had owned the plays. The publication in 1595 of *Locrine*, 'Newly set foorth, overseene and corrected, By *W.S.*' as the title-page describes it, may, if Shakespeare is the man behind the initials, be evidence of further work, seeing an anonymous play into print.

Shakespeare was now demonstrating his consummate ease in a wide range of genres and theatrical techniques: the frenetic farce within a potentially tragic frame of *The Comedy of Errors*; the learned, witty, verbal games and inconclusive ending of *Love's Labour's Lost*; the lyrical virtuosity and sharply personal politics of *Richard II*; the outrageous sexy comedy, romantic love, and tragic conclusion of *Romeo and Juliet*; and the metrical pyrotechnics and supernatural mechanism of *A Midsummer Night's Dream*. There is in this list a sustained experimentation with form, with theatricality, and with language. There was, as well, a new attitude to the materials out of which his plays were created. For *Romeo and Juliet*, for instance, he went back to a work he had used in part for *The Two Gentlemen of Verona*, Arthur Brooke's *Tragical History of Romeus and Juliet* (1562; reprinted 1587), an immensely long poem in fourteeners, turning Brooke's rather dull epic into an exhilarating and immediate drama while mining the original for details to feed into his play. But it is striking, too, that neither *Love's Labour's Lost* nor *A Midsummer Night's Dream* has a single narrative source, something that could have offered

Shakespeare a clear shape for the plot. Both comedies are also concerned with the nature of theatre itself, embedding into their final sequence a performance (the pageant of the Nine Worthies and the play of Pyramus and Thisbe) that both comments on the drama as a whole and analyses audience response. Shakespeare is clearly reflecting on his own art.

Over the next two years, Shakespeare continued to write comedies set in Italy: *The Merchant of Venice* marked the continuing influence of Marlowe, depending on *The Jew of Malta* as *Richard II* had on Marlowe's *Edward II*; *Much Ado about Nothing* turned a traditional trope of mistaken identity into a dark comedy on the social pressures to marry. But he also returned to *Richard II* and began a new cycle of plays, explicitly designed, as the epilogue to *Henry V* would make plain, to connect with his earlier cycle which had dramatized the collapse of rule, empire, and nation after the early death of Henry V. He turned back to the Queen's Men's play *The Famous Victories of Henry V*, with its sharp contrast of the prince's riotous youth and victorious adulthood, as a foundation for a prolonged meditation on the looming threat of succeeding to the crown, on the nature of kingship and the identity of England itself. The two parts of *Henry IV* and *Henry V* created a complete and continuous cycle of eight plays in all, a work of extraordinary ambition and scale, something no English dramatist had attempted before or would attempt again.

But *1 Henry IV* brought him into conflict with a powerful family. In articulating a tension between the world of politics and an alternative culture in which Prince Henry resists the inevitable future call to the throne, Shakespeare originally named the prince's tavern companion Sir John Oldcastle. Whether deliberately or not, the name was guaranteed to offend the family of William Brooke, Lord Cobham, who had been lord chamberlain from 1596 to his death in 1597, for Oldcastle, the Lollard leader revered as a protestant martyr, was Cobham's ancestor. Under pressure from the family the name was changed to Sir John Falstaff, but only after *1 Henry IV* had been performed. Other names were changed in the play: Russell became Peto since the family name of the earls of Bedford was Russell, while Harvey became Bardolph since Sir William Harvey was about to marry the countess of Southampton. The politics of naming continued into *The Merry Wives of Windsor* where Master Ford's original name in his disguise, Brook, while allowing watery puns on 'ford', had to be changed to Broom, again after the first performances: Shakespeare may well have first used Brook as a joke at the expense of Lord Cobham's surname.

Rowe reported that Shakespeare wrote *Merry Wives* at Queen Elizabeth's request, the queen being so pleased with the character of Falstaff that she 'commanded him to continue it for one Play more, and to shew him in Love' (*Works*, ed. Rowe, 1.viii–ix). The anecdote is unlikely to be true, but it is far more probable that the play was performed at the celebrations in May 1597 before the installation into the Order of the Garter of Sir George Carey, now Lord Hunsdon, the son of the founder of the Chamberlain's Men and himself now in the same office after Cobham's death. Where there is neither proof nor likelihood that *A Midsummer Night's Dream* was written for and performed at an aristocratic wedding, as is often suggested, *Merry Wives*, while also performed at The Theatre, was adapted to this specific occasion. The company clearly would have wished to praise their patron and mark his high honour and their playwright used his latest play, capitalizing on the exceptional success of Falstaff in the *Henry IV* plays, to provide an appropriate tribute. Plays could earn companies money and goodwill in more ways than through the box office.

Private tragedy and material success

But the years 1596 and 1597 were also deeply affected by more domestic matters. On 11 August 1596 Hamnet Shakespeare was buried. It is too easy to assume that all expressions of grief in the plays thereafter were a reaction to his son's death, but something of Viola's passionate mourning for the apparent death of her twin brother in *Twelfth Night* could have been generated by the loss of Hamnet, Shakespeare's only male heir. It is not too fanciful to see Shakespeare drawn as a result towards the subject matter of *Hamlet*, where son grieves for father rather than father for son.

Two months later John Shakespeare was granted a coat of arms, about twenty-five years after he had first applied for them, but it was probably William who reactivated the application. It was an opportune moment, for the Garter king of arms, Sir William Dethick, was fairly unscrupulous about entitlement and hence was attacked later by the York herald for granting arms not to John Shakespeare but to 'Shakespear the Player'. The draft spoke eloquently but probably fraudulently of the 'valeant service' done by John's 'late grandfather' for which he was 'advanced & rewarded by the most prudent prince King Henry the seventh'. But it more accurately identified John as an erstwhile bailiff in Stratford (albeit getting the date of office wrong). It also noted that John 'hathe Landes & tenementes of good wealth, & substance 500$^{\text{li.}}$,' (Chambers, 2.19–20). Even allowing for some exaggeration the statement suggests either a remarkable turnaround in John Shakespeare's fortunes or, more probably, an indication of William's rapidly accumulating wealth, enough to make the player and playmaker wish to be able to sign himself as a gentleman. The coat of arms, with gold and silver as its metals, was an expensive option if it was to be reproduced on the bearer's possessions. But the arms are surmounted by an arrogant falcon, punningly displayed shaking its angled spear which, with its silver tip, looks as much like a pen as a weapon. The bird may also be an allusion to the four silver falcons in Southampton's coat of arms. The design and its motto, *Non sancz droict* ('Not without right'), were soon mocked by Jonson whose character Puntarvolo in *Every Man out of his Humour* (Lord Chamberlain's Men, 1599) jeers at Sogliardo, the country clown, by suggesting he should have as his motto 'Not without mustard', an allusion both to Shakespeare's motto and to the yellow colour of his arms.

In 1599 John Shakespeare made an application, probably never approved, to quarter the Arden arms with Shakespeare's and thereby cement the claim to gentility by association with a far more distinguished family. But Dethick's actions were challenged: Brooke, the York herald, identified twenty-three wrongly awarded coats of arms and, though Shakespeare's claim was defended, Shakespeare might never have been confident that the grant of arms had been fair.

Soon afterwards, Shakespeare took another step towards establishing his status and position. While he was in London his wife and children had probably continued to live in Henley Street with his parents; there is no sign that Anne ever moved to London to be with her husband there. In May 1597 Shakespeare bought New Place, reputedly the second largest house in

Stratford, with five gables, ten fireplaces, and a frontage of over 60 feet, together with two barns, two gardens, and two orchards. The price is unclear but was probably in excess of £120. There may have been some rebuilding—a load of stone was sold to the town council in 1598 for 10*d*.—and by February 1598 Shakespeare was listed as living in Chapel Street ward, where New Place was situated, when he, together with many of his neighbours, was shown to be hoarding malt. Shakespeare's store (10 quarters or about 80 bushels) was about the average in the ward but, after three bad harvests, such hoarding was a serious action.

Correspondence in 1598 between two Stratford men, Abraham Sturley and Richard Quiney, shows that they thought of Shakespeare both as 'our countriman' and as someone wealthy enough to be worth Quiney's approaching for a loan of £30 to pay his London debts. In London, Quiney wrote a letter to Shakespeare, in which he is addressed as 'Loveinge Contreyman'; though probably never sent, it is the only surviving piece of correspondence with him. Clearly Shakespeare's finances were sufficient to establish him as a highly visible member of the Stratford community and one seeking to rise further as a local worthy, showing him to have been considered a Stratford resident: Sturley's plan to sell Shakespeare 'some od yardeland or other att Shottri or neare about us' was something that 'would advance him in deede' (Chambers, 2.101–2).

Over subsequent years Shakespeare consolidated his position in Stratford and it was there, rather than in London, that he made his major investments, perhaps because property in Stratford was considered, mistakenly, to be less vulnerable to fire than in London. In May 1602 he paid £320, an enormous sum, for 107 acres of land in Old Town in Stratford, bought from John and

William Combe, and in September 1602 he acquired a cottage in Chapel Lane, probably to extend his land at New Place. In 1605 he paid £440 for a share in the tithes for Stratford, amounting to approximately one-fifth of the total value and worth £60 a year.

Shakespeare in London, 1598–1601

In the course of less than a decade Shakespeare had earned, borrowed, or been given enough to spend nearly £900 in his home town. By comparison, it is not clear what sort of property Shakespeare lived in while in London at this time. Late in 1596 he was known to have been living in the parish of St Helen's, Bishopsgate, by having failed to pay various levies due at this time. His goods were valued in 1598 at a mere £5, a comparatively small sum. The location was reasonably convenient for walking to The Theatre. He had moved away by 1599 and was now resident in the Clink parish in Surrey, in the Liberty. This was conveniently close to the site of the new Globe Theatre where the company was resident for the rest of his career, once they had rebuilt The Theatre on its new site south of the Thames when the lease was up on the land it had occupied. None of this suggests much of a commitment to living in London by comparison with the sustained, substantial, and frequent investment in and around Stratford.

But the move to be near the Globe Theatre marks a new stage in Shakespeare's professional career and it is an apt moment to take stock. He had become a widely known and admired playwright and poet. The *Parnassus* plays, performed by students of St John's College, Cambridge, at the Christmas celebrations between 1598 and 1601, mock Gullio who speaks 'nothinge but pure Shakspeare, and shreds of poetrie that he hath gathered at the theators' and praises 'sweet Mr. Shakspeare!'; Gullio will sleep with 'his Venus, and Adonis under my pillowe' (Chambers, 2.200–01). Poets like Richard Barnfield, John Marston, Robert Tofte, and John Weever referred to Shakespeare's plays and poems in their own poems and epigrams published in 1598 and 1599. In 1598, in *Palladis tamia: Wits Treasury*, Francis Meres praised Shakespeare fulsomely (all Meres's praise is fulsome): 'As *Plautus* and *Seneca* are accounted the best for Comedy and Tragedy among the Latines: so *Shakespeare* among the English is the most excellent in both kinds for the stage', going on to list six comedies and six tragedies (four of which would now be identified as histories) as proof of Shakespeare's status (F. Meres, *Palladis tamia*, fol. 282*r*). In 1600 a collection of quotations, *Belvedere, or, The Garden of the Muses* included over 200 passages from Shakespeare, mostly from *Venus and Adonis*, *Lucrece*, and *Richard II*.

In March 1602 John Manningham, a barrister at the Middle Temple where Shakespeare's *Twelfth Night* had been performed the previous month, noted a bawdy story about Shakespeare and Burbage in his diary; whether true or not, the story (of Shakespeare having sex with a woman who had wanted an assignation with Burbage whom she had fallen for as Richard III) indicates that Shakespeare was a figure to be gossiped about, though Manningham had to remind himself of Shakespeare's first name. Sir George Buck, unsure who had written *George a Greene* (1599), wrote on his copy that Shakespeare had told him it was by 'a minister who ac[ted] the pinner part in it himself' (Honan, 204); Shakespeare's information was probably wrong but Buck saw him as someone worth consulting on such matters. Finally, in this sequence of contacts, Shakespeare's success was sufficient to make one of his colleagues mock him: Jonson's *Every Man out of his Humour* (1599) has a number of satirical allusions to Shakespeare's recent plays as well as to his gentrified status. This amounts to more than a private dig at a friend: Jonson appears to have expected the audience to understand the barbs, yet another sign of Shakespeare's popularity.

Shakespeare's plays were also starting to appear in print both in versions that give unauthorized and often inaccurate versions of the plays and in reasonably carefully prepared versions, the latter often in response to the former: for example the quarto of *Romeo and Juliet* published in 1599, 'Newly corrected, augmented, and amended', in answer to the imperfections of the 1595 quarto. The suspect quartos often bear apparent traces of performance in their more elaborate stage directions. A positive flurry of editions appeared in 1600: *2 Henry IV*, *Henry V*, *The Merchant of Venice*, *A Midsummer Night's Dream*, and *Much Ado about Nothing*, as well as reprints of three other plays and *The Rape of Lucrece*. Some of these published editions of his plays now carried the author's name on their title-pages—for example, *Love's Labour's Lost*, the second quartos of *Richard II* and *Richard III* all published in 1598, or the third quarto of *1 Henry IV* in 1599—another indication of Shakespeare's growing reputation and significance, since playwrights were not usually named on their plays in print.

In 1605 the placing of Shakespeare's name on the title-page of *The London Prodigal*, a play certainly not by Shakespeare, is a further sign that his name was a good marketing ploy; the same (presumably deliberate) misattribution happened with the publication of Thomas Middleton's *A Yorkshire Tragedy* in 1608 (though some have argued that the play is by Shakespeare).

34 Similarly, in 1599 William Jaggard published the second edition of a collection of poems called *The Passionate Pilgrim* (the date of the first edition is uncertain) which the title-page also attributed to Shakespeare, much to Shakespeare's annoyance that Jaggard, as Thomas Heywood noted, 'altogether unknowne to him ... presumed to make so bold with his name' (Schoenbaum, *Documentary Life*, 219). Very little of the collection was by Shakespeare but it included pirated and unattributed printings of three extracts from *Love's Labour's Lost* offered as poems and of two of Shakespeare's sonnets (138 and 144). Meres had noted that 'the sweete wittie soule of *Ovid* lives in mellifluous & hony-tongued *Shakespeare*, witness his *Venus and Adonis*, his *Lucrece*, his sugred Sonnets among his private friends, &c.' (F. Meres, *Palladis tamia*, fols. 281*v*–282*r*). Whenever the sonnets were written, these two at least were by 1599 available in versions Jaggard could use.

Public figure, King's Man

4

Plays, 1598–1601

Having completed the second tetralogy in his history cycle, with the epilogue to *Henry V* gesturing to the earlier sequence ('Which oft our stage hath shown'; epilogue, l. 13), Shakespeare might reasonably have thought he had dramatized enough English history and had made enough use of Holinshed's *Chronicles*. He turned to Roman history, a field he had ignored since *Titus Andronicus* but a rich resource for political analysis of contemporary society. *Julius Caesar* was probably the first play the Chamberlain's Men performed at their new theatre, the Globe, where Thomas Platter, a Swiss traveller, saw it on 21 September 1599. Shakespeare's main source was North's Plutarch—perhaps he had now acquired a copy from Richard Field—and Shakespeare kept closer to his source than ever before, dramatizing Plutarch often simply by turning North's prose into verse. Roman historical tragedy may have been successful but *Julius Caesar*, like *Titus*, was not to be the start of a sequence, though *Antony and Cleopatra* would later take up the story.

Women disguising themselves as young men had been a useful plot device in both *The Two Gentlemen of Verona* and *The Merchant of Venice*. Something, perhaps the expertise of a particularly brilliant boy player, made the prospect of making this transformation especially central to a comedy clearly appealing. In *As You Like It* (1599–1600) and *Twelfth Night* (1601), Shakespeare explored the idea to something approaching its limits. For *As You Like It*, his principal source was Thomas Lodge's prose romance *Rosalynde* (1590) but, where Lodge's work is unequivocally placed in the forest of the Ardennes, Shakespeare's play is set ambiguously in France and in the Forest of Arden that had covered the centre of England and from which his mother's family derived its name. In this play Shakespeare also paid a small tribute to Marlowe as Phoebe remembers the words of the 'Dead shepherd': 'Who ever loved that loved not at first sight?' (III.v, ll. 82–3). *Twelfth Night*'s first recorded performance was at the Middle Temple; John Manningham noted its likeness to Plautus's *Menaechmi* and 'most like and neere to that in Italian called *Inganni*' (Chambers, 2.328).

In both plays Shakespeare made use of the talents of the Chamberlain's Men's latest recruit, Robert Armin, who replaced Will Kemp in 1599; Armin's skills as a singer are clear in Touchstone and Feste, the first signs of the line of fools that Shakespeare wrote for him, far more bitter than those for Kemp.

Between the two comedies Shakespeare wrote *Hamlet*, rewriting the 'Hamlet' play that had been playing on the London stage by 1589 and may have been written by Thomas Kyd. Now lost and probably never printed, the earlier play and its own sources can be presumed to have provided a similar narrative but a simpler one. Nothing in them would have been as complex or provocative as Shakespeare's creation of the prince whose thought processes have been so profoundly influential on Western literature. Whatever else made the writing of *Hamlet* happen at this time, the extraordinary talents of Richard Burbage were a major determinant on the creation of the role, his lifelike acting deeply affecting Shakespeare's portrayal of the prince's mind. But, in creating Ophelia, Shakespeare seems also to have remembered a Stratford event, the inquest into the drowning, just outside Stratford in December 1579, of the aptly named Katherine Hamlett.

Hamlet has its topical references to the work of the boys' companies, the popular rivals to the success of the Chamberlain's Men, but Shakespeare's *Henry V* had made a more direct and political reference in its anticipation of the return of Essex, 'the General of our gracious Empress' (V, chorus, l. 30), from subduing the rebellious Irish during the earl of Tyrone's uprising. But when Essex did return, unexpectedly and without permission, the eventual tension placed Shakespeare and the Chamberlain's Men in danger: Essex's ally Sir Gilly Meyrick and others of Essex's faction paid for the company to perform Shakespeare's *Richard II* two days before Essex's attempt at a coup in February 1601, daring to suggest to the audience that Essex would be Elizabeth's Bolingbroke. The actors claimed later, examined in the dangerous days following the failed coup, that they had argued that the play was 'so old and so long out of use' that 'they shold have small or no Company at yt' (Schoenbaum, *Documentary Life*, 160) but were persuaded to perform it for an extra £2. Shakespeare's play was clearly perceived as dangerous and the scene of Richard's deposition was never included in published versions until the fourth quarto (1608). The performance did no lasting damage to Shakespeare or to the theatre company which continued to be summoned to play at court for the Christmas festivities.

Shakespeare in Stratford, 1601–1609

Other events of 1601 link Shakespeare and Stratford upon Avon. In March Thomas Whittington, who had been shepherd to Shakespeare's father-in-law, made his will, bequeathing to the poor the £2 which Anne Shakespeare had and which William therefore owed to his estate. Quite why the money had been loaned or deposited with Anne is unclear but it seems to indicate Shakespeare's absence from her. On 8 September 1601 John Shakespeare was buried in Stratford. No will survives but William, as the eldest son, would have inherited the house in Henley Street, though, with New Place, he had no need of it: his mother and his sister Joan, who had in the 1590s married William Hart, a hatter, together with her family continued to live there.

Unsurprisingly, most of the documents that speak of Shakespeare in connection with Stratford over the next few years concern legal matters: in spring 1604 he sold malt to a neighbour, Philip Rogers, and subsequently lent him 2*s*.; Rogers repaid 6*s*. and Shakespeare sued for the remainder of the debt, 35*s*. 10*d*. There was another suit for a debt owed by John Addenbrooke: Shakespeare pursued him in the courts from August 1608 to June 1609, seeking £6 plus 24*s*. damages. Clearly Shakespeare was not willing to let such matters drop whether the sums were substantial or not, though in 1608 he may have been short of income with the theatres again shut by plague.

Poems and plays, 1601–1603

Shakespeare's densely enigmatic allegorical poem 'The Phoenix and Turtle' was published in 1601, appended to Robert Chester's *Love's Martyr* in a group, *Poeticall Essaies*, including poems by Marston, Chapman, Jonson, and others, offered as a tribute to Sir John Salusbury with whom Shakespeare has no other known connection. In the following year Shakespeare wrote *Troilus and Cressida*, in part a response to George Chapman's translation of Homer's *Iliad*, a section of which had been published in 1598, and in part an engagement with Chaucer's long poem and Henryson's continuation, the first time Shakespeare had made extensive use of Chaucer since *A Midsummer Night's Dream*. Cynical about sexual desire and war, the play's bleakness may have been aimed at a different audience from that of the Globe—if it was performed at all—since, when it was published in 1609, it carried an epistle identifying it as 'a new play, never stal'd with the Stage, never clapper-clawd with the palmes of the vulger' (*Troilus and Cressida*, 1609, sig. ¶2*r*); the phrase may refer to performance in a space other than the Globe.

The accession of James I brought the Chamberlain's Men an extraordinary honour: soon after arriving in London, James took over patronage of the company, now to be known as the King's Men. For the king's entry into London in May 1604, Shakespeare and the other players, like the members of the Queen's Men, Prince Henry's Men, and many other members of the royal household, were each given four and a half yards of red cloth, possibly to march in the procession or line the route. The King's Men frequently performed at the new court: between November 1604 and October 1605 they played eleven different works, seven of which were by Shakespeare, including new plays such as *Measure for Measure* and *Othello* and older ones such as *The Merchant of Venice* (twice) and *The Merry Wives of Windsor*; between the patent of May 1603 and Shakespeare's death they performed at court on at least 107 occasions.

Yet royal patronage could not solve some of the company's problems: performances at the Globe in 1603–4 had been frequently stopped for lengthy periods because of a sequence of plague, Elizabeth's final illness, public mourning, and further outbreaks of plague. The king gave the company £30 to tide them over while they could not perform. Not until April 1604 was public playing allowed again.

Shakespeare had hardly been idle during this difficult time for the company: *Measure for Measure*, *Othello*, and *All's Well that Ends Well* belong to 1603–4. They follow the ambiguity of genre that characterizes *Troilus and Cressida* which was variously identified as a comedy in the prefatory epistle, a history on the title-page of the quarto of 1609, and a tragedy in the first folio. They share a world of misplaced sexual desire where one body can be substituted for another either unknowingly as in the bed-tricks of *Measure* and *All's Well* or in fantasy as in Iago's report that Cassio had taken Othello's place in the marriage-bed. While *Othello* is a tragedy using the materials of comic cuckoldry, the other two can be wrenched from potential tragedy towards an uncertain comic ending.

In 1605 and 1606 Shakespeare's playwriting energies were spent on unequivocal tragedies: the astonishing sequence of *Timon of Athens*, *King Lear*, *Macbeth*, and *Antony and Cleopatra*. In *Timon*, for the first time since the early stages of his career (depending on exactly when Shakespeare contributed to 'Sir Thomas More'), Shakespeare collaborated with another dramatist, the younger and equally successful Thomas Middleton, the two dividing the play up between them. Middleton was probably also responsible for some of the witches' scenes in *Macbeth* in the only form in which they reached print and he revised *Measure for Measure* in 1621 shortly before it was first printed in the first folio. Shakespeare was not a dramatist who worked in isolation from his fellow playwrights: he was strongly influenced by their plays and by their audiences' responses, just as his work also influenced them. Collaboration became increasingly a part of his playwriting method for the remainder of his career.

Political and other contemporary events affected the plays too. Both *King Lear* and *Macbeth* reflect in some ways the accession of King James: James's concern to unite Scotland and England seems to underpin the division of the kingdom in *Lear*, a warning of the consequences of disunity, while his claim of descent from Banquo is explicitly imaged in *Macbeth* where the witches show Macbeth the line of Banquo's descendants stretching towards James himself. *King Lear* also reflects a recent case in 1603 when Brian Annesley's eldest daughter tried to have her father declared insane and was prevented by the loving care of Annesley's youngest daughter, Cordell.

Yet if all these plays cannot be seen as other than tragedies, they are deliberately 'impure'. As Antony Scoloker commented in 1604 in the epistle to his poem *Diaphantus*: a good poem should be 'like *Friendly Shakespeare's Tragedies*, where the *Commedian* rides, when the *Tragedian* stands on Tip-toe: Faith it should please all, like Prince *Hamlet*' (Chambers, 2.214–15). *Lear* and *Macbeth* are both based on events that, for Shakespeare and his audiences, were the stuff of the chronicles: for both the source material lay in Holinshed; both are histories, as the first published edition of *Lear* (1608) is identified on its title-page. Shakespeare continued to rely on sources that had served him well so far: Holinshed and Plutarch above all but also the repertory of the Queen's Men (for the anonymous *King Leir*), Apuleius's *The Golden Ass*, and Ovid.

Friends and lodgings

Records of Shakespeare's friends and family provide other suggestions about his life at this time. Augustine Phillips, a fellow sharer in the King's Men, died in 1604, leaving 'my ffellowe william Shakespeare a Thirty shillings peece in gould' (Schoenbaum, *Documentary Life*, 204), as he did to other players but naming Shakespeare first. It is reasonable to assume that his fellows in the theatre company were among his closest friends. William Barksted, a minor playwright, wrote warmly of Shakespeare as 'so deere lov'd a neighbor' (Chambers, 2.216). Perhaps to this period too belong the stories, anecdotal but not contradicted by the evidence of surviving comments, of his close friendship and genial rivalry with Jonson.

As becomes apparent from the records of a case in 1612, Shakespeare was living from 1602 to 1604 as a lodger with Christopher Mountjoy and his family in Silver Street in the respectable neighbourhood of Cripplegate. The case provides rare glimpses of Shakespeare's London life in 1602–4 and in 1612. Mountjoy, a French Huguenot refugee, with his wife and daughter, was a successful tiremaker who made wigs and head-dresses; Shakespeare might have met them through the French wife of the printer Richard Field who lived nearby but theatre companies always needed the services of wigmakers and the Lord Chamberlain's Men may have been the connection. Other dramatists lived near, including Jonson, Dekker, Munday, and Field, while

John Heminges and Henry Condell, fellow sharers, were pillars of a local church, St Mary Aldermanbury.

The case of 1612 was brought by Stephen Belott, Mountjoy's former apprentice, who had married Mountjoy's daughter in 1604 and claimed that Mountjoy had failed to pay the dowry promised. Shakespeare was called as a witness and is mentioned by other witnesses. He helped in the marriage negotiations: Mountjoy asked him to encourage Belott to agree to the match and the young couple made their troth-plight in his presence. Six months after the wedding, the Belotts moved out and stayed with George Wilkins, a petty crook who ran a tavern and a brothel. Wilkins was also a writer whose work included a play and a novella, *The Painful Adventures of Pericles Prince of Tyre* (1608), which combines material from Twine's romance *The Pattern of Painful Adventures* (reprinted in 1607) and from Shakespeare's *Pericles*, written in 1607, probably in collaboration with Wilkins who may have contributed the first two acts. Mrs Mountjoy died in October 1608 and the Belotts returned to Silver Street. Arguments continued and Belott sued in 1612 for the unpaid £60 dowry and £200 to be included in Mountjoy's will.

Shakespeare was one of three witnesses examined on 11 May 1612. His deposition brings the closest record of Shakespeare speaking, albeit through the court style of the examiner's clerk. Shakespeare attested that Belott was, in his view, 'A very good and industrious servant' who 'did well and honestly behave himselfe', though he also said that Mountjoy had not 'confesse[d] that he hath gott any great proffitt and comodytye' from Belott's service. He also deposed that the Mountjoys showed Belott 'great good will and affecceon' and that Mrs Mountjoy 'did sollicitt and entreat [him] to move and perswade

[Belott] to effect the said marriadge and accordingly [he] did'. On the matter of money Shakespeare could not remember (or chose not to remember) how large the marriage portion was to have been, nor whether there was to have been a sum in Mountjoy's will, nor 'what Implementes and necessaries of houshold stuffe' Mountjoy gave Belott as part of the marriage settlement (Schoenbaum, *Records*, 25). Further witnesses were examined on 19 June but Shakespeare, though named in the margin of the interrogatories, did not depose again.

In the event the matter was referred to the elders of the French church, who ordered Mountjoy to pay Belott 20 nobles; but Mountjoy, who had fathered two bastards and was excommunicated for his dissolute life, never paid. Whatever the neighbourhood may have been, the Mountjoys were hardly the respectable family they might at first have appeared. The case is trivial enough but it shows Shakespeare caught up in the kind of arguments over money and marriage that figured in many plays of the period.

Events in Shakespeare's family in Stratford in this period balanced good and bad news. In May 1606 his daughter Susanna was listed with other residents of Stratford for refusing to take holy communion at Easter, perhaps a sign that she might be a covert Catholic since such actions were bound to be noticed in the tense aftermath of the Gunpowder Plot. Susanna married in June 1607; her husband, the physician John Hall (1574/5?–1635), was known to be strongly protestant in his faith. There appears to have been a substantial marriage settlement in which Shakespeare settled on Susanna 105 acres of his land in Old Stratford, probably retaining a life interest in it; it amounts to a very valuable dowry. Shakespeare's younger brother Edmund had become a player, following his eldest brother to London, where both he and his infant son died in 1607; William may well have been the person who paid 20*s*. for his brother's burial in St Saviour's, Southwark, 'with a forenoone knell of the great bell' (Schoenbaum, *Documentary Life*, 26). In February 1608 Shakespeare became a grandfather with the birth of Elizabeth Hall. In September of that year his mother died.

Plays, poems, and profits

5

Plays and Sonnets, 1607–1609

In the meantime, Shakespeare was developing new forms for his drama. *Pericles* marked a new departure, a drama whose narrative spreads to and fro across the Mediterranean, with a chorus, the poet John Gower whose poem *Confessio amantis* is one of the play's sources, returned from the grave to tell the tale. From the finality of losing the beloved daughter at the end of *King Lear* to the possibility of a family being reunited at the end of *Pericles* is an enormous distance. *Pericles* was the only play largely written by Shakespeare not to be included in the 1623 first folio but it appeared in a quarto edition in 1608. Its immediate popularity may be indicated by the presence of the French and Venetian ambassadors at a performance in 1608.

If the play marked the start of a new phase in Shakespeare's writing, he made a last exploration of tragedy: *Coriolanus*, once again derived from Plutarch, is his fiercest study of the politics of the state and its citizens, spurred on by the immediate threat of the midlands uprising of 1607–8, a series of outbreaks of popular unrest caused by bad harvests and inflationary food prices. The riots occurred close to Stratford and William Combe, from whom Shakespeare had bought the land in Old Stratford in 1602, warned Lord Salisbury of the risk of sedition.

By 1609 about half of Shakespeare's plays had appeared in print. His long narrative poems continued to be reprinted. In 1609 Thomas Thorpe published *Shake-speares Sonnets*, printed by George Eld who printed the first quarto of *Troilus and Cressida* in the same year. The foregrounding of Shakespeare's name in the very title of the volume suggests that it may well have been authorized by Shakespeare, who could have sold the sequence to Thorpe for publication; the frequent closures of the theatres yet again because of plague in 1607–9 could have encouraged him to find another source of income. Thomas Heywood indicated in 1612 that Shakespeare's annoyance with the earlier unauthorized publication of some of the sonnets in *The Passionate Pilgrim* had made him take action: 'hee to doe himselfe right, hath since published them in his owne name' (Schoenbaum, *Documentary Life*, 219).

The *Sonnets* were prefaced by an enigmatic dedication (with each word followed by a period) signed with Thorpe's initials, mimicking the form of Ben Jonson's dedication of *Volpone* to the universities (published by Thorpe in 1607): 'To the onlie begetter of these ensuing sonnets Mr W. H. all happinesse and that eternitie promised by our ever-living poet wisheth the well-wishing adventurer in setting forth.' Thorpe included 154 sonnets, following them with the long poem 'A Lover's Complaint'. One of the sonnets may date back to his courtship of Anne Hathaway in 1582; Meres had spoken of his 'sugred Sonnets' circulating in manuscript in 1598; a few had been printed in 1599. But when the bulk of them and 'A Lover's Complaint' were written is a matter for argument. So too are the identities of Mr W. H., who may or may not be the young man to whom most of the sonnets are directed, of the 'dark lady' to whom others are aimed, and of the rival poet who appears in the sequence. Shakespeare, the consummate dramatist, may of course be constructing a drama set out in sonnets without any real figures behind it, but if the poems do tell of events in Shakespeare's life the identities of the participants come to matter greatly.

None of the many attempts at identifying the dark lady or the rival poet are finally convincing. But the case for the young man's being William Herbert, third earl of Pembroke, is more thorough and effective, even if there is a strong counter-claim that 'Mr W. H.' deliberately reverses the initials of Henry Wriothesley, third earl of Southampton, who was Shakespeare's patron in the early 1590s. Shakespeare had little known contact with Herbert, though Herbert and his brother were the dedicatees of the first folio in 1625 and praised there for having 'prosequuted both [Shakespeare's plays], and their Authour living, with so much favour' (sig. $^{\pi}$ A2*r*).

The sonnet sequence begins with a group of seventeen poems, apparently commissioned by the young man's family, that attempt to persuade him to marry and leave versions of himself behind in his children; Herbert had repeatedly refused proposed marriages and it is tempting to date these poems to his seventeenth birthday in 1597, perhaps the ones to which Meres referred. Equally well, if this part of the sequence is earlier than 1597, they could have been written to Southampton. In the absence of any significant external evidence, tests of vocabulary tend to suggest that some of the sonnets belong to the mid-1590s, while other internal indications, including possible allusions to the death of Elizabeth, suggest a date about 1603, when 'A Lover's Complaint' is most likely to have been written as a deliberate coda to the sequence. There is no reason to assume that the sequence was written at one time, nor that its differing segments were originally intended to belong together. Most of the poems, with their account of homoerotic desire between the older poet and a younger and unfaithful man (sonnets 1–126), the counter-attractions of heterosexual desire (127–152), and a continual return to self-humiliation, self-loathing, and sexual disgust, may well have been revised. All one can be sure of is that the poems could not have reached their final form as a sequence, ending with the 'Complaint', until at least 1603 and it is just as likely that they were finally revised shortly before publication. Perhaps the two periods of plague and closure provided Shakespeare with opportunities and reasons to work on his sonnets.

In the whole outpouring of sonnets in England in the period, only Richard Barnfield, in *Cynthia* (1595), wrote poems directed to a man. The *Sonnets* in their repeated punning on Shakespeare's first name make the embedding of the poet himself into the sequence plain. Their explicit homoeroticism suggests that Shakespeare's sexuality was consciously bisexual in its desires, though the modern concept of bisexuality and one appropriate to Shakespeare's lifetime may be significantly different. Whether Shakespeare's homoerotic desires led to or were connected with sexual acts with the young man or indeed any other man is far from clear. Read as biographical, they also make plain that fidelity to Anne was not something Shakespeare was much concerned about, though adulterous sex with the 'dark lady' induced deep shame. Whatever their biographical secrets, the poems have an emotional intensity and poetic complexity that make them among Shakespeare's greatest achievements.

50 Plays for the Blackfriars

In 1608 the King's Men had acquired the lease of the Blackfriars Theatre, an indoor playhouse with a far smaller capacity than the Globe and with far higher admission prices; they acted there from the autumn of 1609. The company played in both venues but Blackfriars was by far the more prestigious. With its greater range of stage machinery, its increased use of music, its habitual division of plays into acts (with music between the acts), and its narrower social range of audience, Blackfriars offered Shakespeare a set of new challenges that he responded to in *The Winter's Tale*, *Cymbeline*, and *The Tempest*, and in his final collaborations with John Fletcher. It appears that Shakespeare was writing plays less frequently than earlier, perhaps now no more than one a year. *The Winter's Tale*, *Cymbeline*, and *The Tempest* belong to the years 1609–11 but the exact order in which they were written is impossible to determine, for all that critics prefer to see a simple sequence according to their own preference for a linear dramaturgical development. Shakespeare turned, as for *Pericles*, to the materials of prose romance narrative, for *The Winter's Tale* using Greene's old tale *Pandosto* (1588). All three play self-conscious games with narrative and its amenability to dramatic form: *The Winter's Tale* is broken-backed, something it shares with *Timon of Athens*, moving from compressed urban tragedy to leisurely pastoral comedy before returning redemptively to the location of its tragic phase; *Cymbeline* ostentatiously foregrounds the long sequence of its own multiple revelations that lead to the drama's resolution, as if teasing the audience to find it merely comic; *The Tempest* uses Prospero's magic to achieve compression into three hours on a metamorphic island. All three are particularly aware of their artifice and of the playwright's own art. If they seem to belong only to the world of romance, they are also full of topicality: *Cymbeline*'s movement to Milford Haven harks back to Richmond's landing to overthrow Richard III, and the play is full of comment on King James's vision of Britain as a newly united nation; *The Tempest* plays on the colonizing of America and the encounters with the New World transposed into the Mediterranean. The clashes of worlds, old and new, ancient and modern, near and far, search for new unities.

The style of these plays connects with the drama that Francis Beaumont and John Fletcher were writing at the same time, though the direction of influence is far from clear. Certainly Shakespeare found a new and systematic collaboration with Fletcher desirable and satisfactory, for his next three plays were shared with the younger dramatist who had already written, probably in 1611, a sequel to *The Taming of the Shrew* as *The Woman's Prize, or, The Tamer Tamed.* As with so many contemporary examples of collaboration it is difficult to be sure of the precise shares: each play is perfectly coherent in performance. 'Cardenio', based on an episode in *Don Quixote*, was never printed but a manuscript, now lost, was claimed by Lewis Theobald to be the source for his play *The Double Falsehood* (1728) which shows strong traces of Fletcher in its style. After a prolonged break from the genre, Shakespeare and Fletcher returned to the now unfashionable mode of English history with *Henry VIII*, known to contemporaries as *All is True.* Its worries about competing politics and nostalgia for the optimism at the birth of Elizabeth testify to a cultural nervousness. Finally, if the assumed sequence of the plays is correct, came *The Two Noble Kinsmen*, a return to the chivalric world of Chaucer's 'Knight's tale' but coupled with an unnerving depiction of obsessive desire. Least known of all his work, Shakespeare's final collaborative plays show him continuing to experiment, returning to familiar topics but always in unfamiliar ways.

Lyrics, occasional poems, and revising

Following Shakespeare's writings chronologically has obscured two important kinds of work. The first is difficult to determine: a number of lyrics and occasional epigrams have been attributed to Shakespeare but there is little hard evidence for any of them. There are epitaphs on people, with some of whom Shakespeare had a known or possible connection—for example, the verses on John Combe which were claimed to have been on his monument in Holy Trinity Church in Stratford, or the one on Elias James, a brewer who worked close to the Globe Theatre—and with some of whom there is no known link. It is not even certain that Shakespeare wrote the lines that appeared on his own grave, though they were recorded as his by the mid-seventeenth century. It is, though, probable that he wrote some occasional verse, whether songs, epigrams, or epitaphs. In March 1613 he certainly composed the *impresa* (an allegorical insignia with a motto) carried by the earl of Rutland at the king's accession day tilt; he was paid 44*s*., as was Richard Burbage for painting and making it. It is a rare moment linking Shakespeare directly with court events; unlike Ben Jonson, for instance, Shakespeare wrote masques as part of his plays, not for the court, and, though his plays were often performed at court, he was never one of the writers working for court circles.

The second kind of work is Shakespeare's repeated revising and rewriting of his plays. With the plays being part of the stock repertory of the Chamberlain's Men/King's Men, Shakespeare would have had repeated opportunities to reconsider his work. For some plays there is occasional evidence of revision in the stages of the original composition evident in the single text that reached print: a passage repeated with variants in *Love's Labour's Lost*, for instance, seems to show Shakespeare's first and second thoughts for the speech. But for a number of plays that were printed both in quarto and in the first folio, the variants often indicate large- and small-scale revision. Characters' roles are expanded (for example, Emilia in *Othello*); speeches are rethought; lines are added here and there to produce different echoes and connections; lines, speeches, and whole scenes are deleted to alter the dramatic form and the theatrical pacing. In the cases of *King Lear* and *Hamlet* the alterations between the versions are so substantial as to suggest that each survives as two rather significantly different plays, a quarto and a folio text. Texts in the theatre are often unstable entities; actors change lines they dislike and playwrights alter in response to the experience of rehearsal and production. Shakespeare is unlikely to have made the changes only once; rather, many plays, particularly the most popular ones, are likely to have undergone continual alteration over the years, but leaving only two snapshots of the long process, from first composition through years of performances, surviving in the printed texts.

The last years

In 1613, at the very end of his playwriting career, Shakespeare made a substantial investment in property in London, buying the gatehouse of the old Dominican priory in Blackfriars, where the Blackfriars Theatre was located, for £140. Burbage had also bought property in the area and Shakespeare's purchase may have been simply an investment, since one John Robinson was a tenant there in 1616. But the gatehouse was large enough for Shakespeare to have let part of it and used the rest himself. Wherever he was living in London after leaving the Mountjoys, he could have been in the Blackfriars gatehouse from 1613. Shakespeare paid £80 of the purchase immediately and mortgaged the remainder. Though he was the purchaser, the property was held by him with three others as trustees: John

Heminges of the King's Men, William Johnson, the landlord of the Mermaid Tavern, and John Jackson, possibly the husband of the sister-in-law of Elias James the brewer. The effect may well have been, whether by Shakespeare's design or not, to exclude Anne Shakespeare from having a widow's claim on a third share of the property for her life, her dower right, unless Shakespeare survived the other trustees.

The King's Men remained successful: at the celebrations for the marriage of James I's daughter to the elector palatine in February 1613 they performed fourteen plays, four of which were by Shakespeare (including the not exactly propitious *Othello*). But in June 1613, during a performance of Shakespeare's *Henry VIII*, the Globe Theatre burnt down after some of the stuff shot out of a small cannon, for a sound effect, lodged in the thatch. The sharers decided to rebuild at the cost of over £1400, each sharer contributing between £50 and £60. Shakespeare had certainly sold his share in the company by the time he made his will in 1616; this may have been a good moment to get out.

In 1709 Nicholas Rowe suggested that Shakespeare spent his last years 'in Ease, Retirement, and the Conversation of his Friends... and is said to have spent some Years before his Death at his native *Stratford*' (*Works*, ed. Rowe, 1.xxxv). But, though the story has taken permanent hold, there is no evidence for Shakespeare's having retired to Stratford. In November 1614 Thomas Greene, Stratford's town clerk from 1603 to 1617, who repeatedly refers to Shakespeare as his cousin, was in London and noted that, Shakespeare 'commyng yesterday to towne I went to see him howe he did' (Schoenbaum, *Documentary Life*, 231). Where Shakespeare came from he does not say—it might well have been Stratford—but Shakespeare still came to London. Greene had been at Middle Temple when *Twelfth Night* was performed there and, with his wife and his children, Anne and William (perhaps the Shakespeares had stood godparents to them), were living in New Place in 1609.

Events in Stratford continued to involve Shakespeare, whether he was there or not. He was one of seventy-one Stratford citizens who subscribed to contribute to the cost of promoting a bill in parliament for the repair of roads, being named first, added in the margin, after the town's officials. A visiting preacher was entertained at New Place in 1614, though it is not clear whether Shakespeare was there at the time. There were family sadnesses too: two of his brothers died, Gilbert in February 1612 and Richard in February 1613, leaving only William and his sister Joan alive in that generation. In July 1613 his daughter Susanna brought a case in the bishop's consistory court that John Lane, a wild young man, had slandered her with an accusation of adultery with Rafe Smith and of having gonorrhoea; she won.

There was a local crisis too that affected Shakespeare. William Combe was the son of the William Combe from whom Shakespeare had bought the land in Old Stratford, and cousin of John Combe who left Shakespeare £5 in his will in 1614. Combe and Arthur Mainwaring, steward to Lord Ellesmere, wanted to enclose land at Welcombe from which Shakespeare and Thomas Greene had tithe income. The Stratford corporation opposed the enclosure. Shakespeare covenanted with Mainwaring's agent to be compensated, along with Greene, 'for all such losse detriment & hinderance' consequent on the enclosure (Schoenbaum, *Documentary Life*, 231). Greene's notes on his conversation with Shakespeare in London in November 1614 showed that Shakespeare knew how much land was intended to be enclosed and that compensation would be fixed the following April. Neither Shakespeare nor his son-in-law, John Hall, believed that the enclosure would go ahead. In December the corporation wrote to Shakespeare and Mainwaring to explain their opposition, not least because a fire in July 1613 had left many residents homeless. Combe's men began enclosing in the same month, but the ditch was filled in by women and children. Combe tried bribing Greene unsuccessfully. The struggle dragged on for years until Combe more or less abandoned his plans. Shakespeare's position in all this seems consistent: he was far more concerned to safeguard his income than to protect the townspeople's rights.

Death and memorials

6

Shakespeare's will and death

In January 1616 Shakespeare summoned his lawyer, Francis Collins, to draft his will. The decision was probably provoked by the impending marriage of his other daughter, Judith, to Thomas Quiney, son of Richard Quiney who had sought a loan from Shakespeare in 1598. Thomas was five years younger than Judith and Shakespeare had good reason to distrust him. The marriage took place in February 1616 in the middle of Lent without a special licence, an ecclesiastical offence for which Quiney was excommunicated. But, far more seriously, in March, Margaret Wheeler died giving birth to Quiney's child. Quiney admitted fornication in the ecclesiastical court and was ordered to do public penance, but paid a fine of 5*s*. instead. The first of the three pages of the will was revised late in March, apparently taking account of his son-in-law's crimes by altering the bequests to Judith.

Perhaps nothing in Shakespeare's plays has provoked quite as much commentary as his will (Chambers, 2.170–74). The three pages with their many corrections and interlineations seem full of afterthoughts and adjustments. Shakespeare's first concern is with Judith who would immediately inherit £100 and a further £50 in return for giving up her rights in a copyhold in Rowington to her sister and a further £150 in three years' time; if she were to die before then and without issue, the money would go to Shakespeare's granddaughter Elizabeth Hall and his sister, Joan Hart. But Judith would only receive the interest on the second tranche if she were married, unless her husband matched the capital sum. Thomas Quiney is never named and the will's phrase about 'such husbond as she shall att thend of the saied three Yeares be marryed unto' at the very least suggests that she might be married to someone other than Quiney by then.

Shakespeare moved on to take especial care of his sister. In the event, Joan's husband, William Hart, died in April 1616, a week before Shakespeare; but she was clearly in need of help. She received £20, his clothes, and the house in Henley Street during her lifetime at a peppercorn rent; £5 went to each of Joan's three sons. Shakespeare's plate was to go to his granddaughter Elizabeth except 'my brod silver & gilt bole' which went to Judith. Shakespeare left £10 to the poor of Stratford, not a particularly large sum given his wealth and the fact that his lawyer would receive £13 6*s*. 8*d*.; his sword went to Thomas Combe and there were other bequests to local friends. He had been going to leave a small sum to Richard Tyler but Tyler's name is deleted for some reason. There were extra bequests to buy rings to Hamlet Sadler, his godson William Walker, and others. Of his 'ffellowes' in the King's Men, Shakespeare remembered, belatedly and in an interlineation, only three—Burbage, Heminges, and Condell—who would each receive 26*s*. 8*d*. for rings. Almost everything else went to Susanna, some in reconfirmation of the marriage settlement but the rest carefully tied up for the future for any sons she might have (up to seven) and only then to

Elizabeth Hall or thereafter to Judith and her future sons. The generosity to Susanna and therefore to John Hall who were also appointed executors is offset by the tightly limited bequests to Judith. There is no mention of books or papers in the will—hardly a surprise since these would be part of his household goods which the Halls would receive; they did not need special reference.

Interlineated as an afterthought on the third page is the only reference to Anne, like Quiney unnamed: 'Item I gyve unto my wief my second best bed with the furniture'. The second-best bed may well have been the marriage bed with the best bed reserved for guests. But it is not clear whether in Stratford Anne would automatically have received the widow's dower rights of one-third of the estate; there were sharp regional variations in practice. Certainly the will's silence prevents her having control over any part of the estate. Other wills were far more explicit: Burbage's 'wellbeloved' wife was his executor; Henry Condell's 'wellbeloved' wife received all his property (E. A. J. Honigmann and S. Brock, *Playhouse Wills, 1558–1642*, 1993, 113, 157). The lack in Shakespeare's will of even a conventional term of endearment, of specific and substantial bequests to Anne, or even of the right to continue living in New Place amounts to a striking silence.

On 23 April 1616 Shakespeare died. John Ward, a clergyman living in Stratford in the 1660s, recorded that 'Shakespear, Drayton, and Ben Jhonson had a merry meeting, and itt seems drank too hard, for Shakespear died of a feavour there contracted' (Chambers, 2.250). The story is not impossible but quite what Shakespeare died from is unknown. He was buried two days later in Holy Trinity, inside the church rather than in the churchyard because his purchase of an interest in the

Stratford tithes in 1605 made him a lay rector. The epitaph, possibly written by himself, warning future generations to leave his bones where they lay, was inscribed on the grave, though the grave may not originally have been where the stone is now placed. Anne lived until 1623 (she was buried on 8 August) but her tombstone makes no mention of her husband, and refers to only one daughter; Judith seems to have been ignored.

The Stratford monument, the Droeshout engraving, and other portraits

Anne probably lived to see the monument to her husband in Holy Trinity Church (which was certainly in place by 1623) but she could not have seen the publication of *Mr William Shakespeares Comedies, Histories, & Tragedies* (the first folio) in November or December of the same year. The monument and the title-page to the volume are the only two images of Shakespeare to have an especially strong likelihood of accuracy. The former was made by Geerart Janssen, a sculptor of Dutch descent; his father was also a sculptor who had made the tomb for the earl of Southampton, father of Shakespeare's patron. The Janssens had also worked for the earls of Rutland and were commissioned in 1618 to make a tomb for the fifth earl, by the sixth earl for whom Shakespeare and Burbage had made their *impresa* in 1613. Depicted as a writer, his mouth open as he prepares to write on the paper under his left hand (though the earliest reproduction, by Dugdale in 1656, dispensed with pen and paper), the Shakespeare of the monument has seemed too corpulent for some admirers, as if genius should be lean. It is precisely its unremarkable appearance, described by Dover Wilson as that of a 'self-satisfied pork-butcher' (Schoenbaum, *Records*, 161), that has convinced others of its accuracy. Frequently restored and recoloured—it was painted white in 1793 at Edmond Malone's urging but returned to what were assumed to be the original colours in 1861—the monument was used by the Flower brewery in Stratford as the trademark to sell its products and plaster casts derived from it were widely distributed. It is still the representation of Stratford's view of Shakespeare.

London's view may be embodied in the image on the title-page of the collection of his plays. The engraving has usually been ascribed to Martin Droeshout the younger, aged only twenty-one when the portrait was made in 1622, probably initially for separate distribution and not as part of the forthcoming volume, but its old-fashioned style might possibly have been the work of his uncle, Martin Droeshout the elder (*d. c*.1642), a Flemish protestant refugee in England and a leading member of the Painter–Stainers' Company in London at this time. This image of Shakespeare with its massive dome of a forehead 'like another dome of St Paul's' (A. L. Rowse, quoted in Schoenbaum, *Records*, 171), concealing, it seems to imply, a brain of disproportionate size, has become one of the most potent icons of Western culture, the very essence of the originating author making his presence visible in connection with his works. It can now be found on thousands of products, from tea towels to plastic bags to the British Library's computer catalogue (until 1999), but the mere idea of placing an image of an author on the title-page of a collection was unusual. There was no engraving of Ben Jonson on the title-page of Jonson's folio edition of his *Works*, published in 1616. But Jonson's poem on the Shakespeare portrait, placed to face it opposite the title-page, identifies both the image's accuracy and its inadequacy:

> O, could he but have drawne his wit
> As well in brasse, as he hath hit
> His face; the Print would then surpasse
> All that was ever writ in brasse.

The image exists in three distinct states in different copies of the first folio and the deteriorating plate was used for the subsequent folios as well. It was the source for William Marshall's engraving for the pirated 1640 edition of Shakespeare's poems and William Faithorne's for the 1655 edition of *The Rape of Lucrece*. Thereafter it became fair game for anyone seeking to represent their version of Shakespeare.

Droeshout's engraving is also the source of the 'Flower' portrait, now owned by the Royal Shakespeare Company, which was found in 1840 and was then claimed to be Droeshout's source. Its date is unclear and it has now been shown to be a nineteenth-century forgery. It reflects the often desperate desire to find authentic images of Shakespeare, like the Ashbourne portrait (not of Shakespeare at all), first 'identified' in 1847, and the Ely Palace portrait, also a supposed source for Droeshout, discovered in 1845. Others were 'found' earlier, like the Felton or Burdett-Coutts portrait exhibited in 1792 or the Janssen portrait engraved in 1770; still others surfaced much later like the Grafton portrait, unknown before 1907, or the Sanders portrait, publicized in 2001. Sometimes a known image is, for a while, claimed to be of Shakespeare, like the Hilliard miniature which Leslie Hotson identified as Shakespeare in 1977. None of these is likely to be a portrait of Shakespeare independent of the Droeshout engraving or the Stratford bust; many are not even images of Shakespeare at all. Their claims are no more probable than that the plaster cast now in Darmstadt is indeed Shakespeare's death mask.

The only exception to this long succession of dubious manifestations of the bardolatrous desire to have a new image to worship is the Chandos portrait, the most probable of all the claimed portraits. Its provenance secure from 1719 (though earlier owners may have included the actor Thomas Betterton), it eventually came to the Chandos family and was then given by Lord Ellesmere in 1856 as the first picture (still catalogued as 'NPG 1') to enter the infant National Portrait Gallery, an image of the nation's greatest writer with which symbolically to found a collection of British historical portraits. It was copied by Kneller for John Dryden by 1694, Dryden responding with a poem to Kneller praising Shakespeare's 'Majestick Face' (Dryden, 'To Sir Godfrey Kneller', *The Poems and Fables of John Dryden*, ed. James Kinsley, 1962, 497). A version by Michael van der Gucht was part of the frontispiece of Rowe's edition of 1709 and the Tonson family's sequence of Shakespeare editions through the eighteenth century (until 1767) continued the tradition. Indeed, since the Tonsons' address from 1710 was a building they named 'Shakespeare's Head', the Chandos portrait became their commercial trademark. It has been reproduced at least as often as the Droeshout engraving.

Probably painted by John Taylor about 1610 the Chandos image is, if genuine, the only one made before Shakespeare's death. Its swarthiness has created anxieties among some who saw it as too Italian or too Jewish to be Shakespeare's true likeness. Its fashionable gold earring has troubled others at times when male dress was more restrained. It has, more often, been seen as a more acceptably realistic image than either the Droeshout engraving or the Stratford monument.

Elegies and influence on contemporaries

Shakespeare's death prompted at least one elegy: a poem, usually ascribed to William Basse, circulated quite widely in manuscript but was not printed until 1633 (when it appeared as by John Donne who may well have been the author). The poem's recommendation that Spenser, Chaucer, and Beaumont should move up in their tombs in Westminster Abbey to leave space for Shakespeare was well enough known for Jonson to allude to it and refute it in his poem 'To the memory of my beloved, the author Mr. William Shakespeare: and what he hath left us' prefixed to the first folio. For Jonson, Shakespeare was:

> … a Moniment, without a tombe
> And art alive still, while thy Booke doth live,
> And we have wits to read, and praise to give.
> (W. Shakespeare, *Comedies, Histories, & Tragedies*, 1623, sig. $^{\pi}$A4*r*)

Although Shakespeare's death was not marked by a published collection of verses, an exceptionally rare public effusion for any writer, his work continued to be powerfully influential on contemporary audiences and dramatists alike. Far from his plays and poems coming quickly to be seen as old-fashioned and outdated, references and allusions to his plays and poems in commonplace books, poems, and other writings certainly did not stop with the end of his career. Shakespeare's spectators and readers remained fascinated by his work.

As significantly, just as Shakespeare himself continually reworked scenes, characters, speeches, and thoughts from his own and others' earlier plays into his latest writing, so other playwrights turned to Shakespeare as a major resource for their own development. The late plays and the final collaborations with Fletcher spawned dozens of imitations, as if Shakespeare had defined the age's style. But there were quotations and allusions in numerous plays, ranging from the deliberately resonant to the probably unconscious, as if writing plays now necessitated engagement with his work in a playwriting culture effectively in part defined and even dominated by Shakespeare. When, like Desdemona, the heroine in Webster's *The Duchess of Malfi* (printed 1623) revives for a few moments after being strangled, or when Cornelia in his *The White Devil* (1612) madly distributes herbs like Ophelia, when Middleton's and Rowley's *The Changeling* (performed 1622) has an honest villain like Iago and their Beatrice, like Shakespeare's in *Much Ado*, asks a man to undertake a killing each woman is unable to do for herself, then these great younger contemporaries are, consciously or not, deriving their effects from Shakespeare. But such recycling of Shakespearian materials is not in any way restricted to the work of the best: out of dozens of possible examples, one might note a drama of lovers from rival families in Thomas May's *The Heir* (acted 1620), a murderer who cannot wash the blood from his hands in William Heminges's *The Jews' Tragedy* (*c*.1626), or a play put on for royalty by workers whose leading actor wants to play all the parts in Thomas Rawlins's *The Rebellion* (printed 1640). Shakespeare was not the only dramatist to affect those who came after, nor is it sensible to try to quantify resonances, borrowings, and allusions to determine whether Shakespeare was more or less influential than Jonson. But his plays were already becoming a central store of possibilities which dramatists could raid, largely without acknowledgement.

The first folio

Where the raiders could find the work changed substantially with the decision to publish something approximating to a volume of Shakespeare's collected plays. In 1616 the publication of Ben Jonson's *Works* marked the first occasion on which the plays of a vernacular dramatist had been collected. Jonson had spent years on the volume and had included poems and prose works as well. The project to gather Shakespeare's work may have begun with John Heminges and Henry Condell, Shakespeare's fellow actors, though it is tempting to imagine that Shakespeare's bequest of money for rings to them in his will signalled that the plan was Shakespeare's own.

The planning may have been accelerated, and may even have been provoked, by Thomas Pavier's unauthorized publication in 1619 of a group of quartos of plays ostensibly by Shakespeare. Pavier and his printer William Jaggard included two plays certainly not by Shakespeare, *Sir John Oldcastle Part 1* (first printed as Shakespeare's in 1600) and *A Yorkshire Tragedy*, and one other, *Pericles*, that would not be part of the first folio. Some of the title-pages had false dates; all were reprints of previously published plays. Most significantly, the collection of ten plays was sold as a set and the Stationers' Company responded to the lord chamberlain's complaint, presumably instigated by the King's Men as owners of the plays, to prohibit publication of their repertory without their consent.

The publication of a folio of Shakespeare's plays was ambitious and expensive. While Heminges and Condell signed the volume's dedication to the earl of Pembroke, who was lord chamberlain, and his younger brother, and were also the authors of the prefatory letter 'To the great Variety of Readers', they were not necessarily the folio's editors, in the modern sense of the word. The cost of the publishing was, as the volume's colophon indicated, the responsibility of William Jaggard and his son Isaac, Edward Blount, John Smethwick, and William Apsley. The publishers needed to secure the printing rights to a number of plays that had already appeared and Smethwick and Apsley, who owned the rights to four and two plays respectively, may have become involved for that reason.

There were thirty-six plays in the volume: eighteen had never been printed before (including, for instance, *Julius Caesar*, *Twelfth Night*, *Macbeth*, *Antony and Cleopatra*, and *The Tempest*) and sixteen of these were acquired from the King's Men themselves. Isaac Jaggard and Edward Blount entered their rights in sixteen plays in the Stationers' register in November 1623, shortly before the volume appeared, including in their list *Antony and Cleopatra*, which Blount had entered in 1608 but never printed. The publication syndicate had to negotiate with seven other stationers for the rights to other plays. News of the planned folio may have encouraged the reprinting of a number of Shakespeare plays in the early 1620s and the first publication of *Othello* in 1622. Problems over rights may have been the cause of the delay in printing *Troilus and Cressida*, which is not named on the contents page (three copies of the volume without the play survive); though originally intended to follow *Romeo and Juliet*, it was in the end placed ambiguously between the histories and the tragedies, either the last of the former or first of the latter. Of the plays which subsequent bibliographers would assign substantially or significantly to Shakespeare, only collaborative plays (*Pericles*, *The Two Noble Kinsmen*, 'Cardenio', and *Edward III*) were missing.

Printing began early in 1622 and took nearly two years. The compositors' copy came from a variety of sources: for example, scribal copies made by Ralph Crane and others from Shakespeare's manuscripts; quartos annotated by reference to manuscript playbooks used at the theatre; the playbooks themselves; and Shakespeare's 'foul papers'. Having decided not to include Shakespeare's poems (which were not reunited with the plays in any edition until 1790), the editor(s) chose to arrange the volume unconventionally by genre and to allow the genres to be the volume's title: *Mr. William Shakespeare's Comedies,*

Histories, & Tragedies. Ben Jonson's naming his volume as his 'works' had attracted some mockery, but the editorial choice of genre as the controlling taxonomy for Shakespeare straitjackets some plays awkwardly. Some had been published with other generic definitions—for example, *Richard II* and *Richard III* had both been published as tragedies, not histories; *King Lear* as history, not tragedy. The folio's organization would cast a long shadow over centuries of analysis.

Within the genre of history the plays, which included only English histories (not British or Roman ones), were arranged by chronological order of reign. Comedies and tragedies were fairly randomly sequenced. None of the ordering reflected the chronology of composition or performance, leaving, again, much confusion and sheer hard work to come.

But the choice of format, for all Jonson's precedent, was crucial, giving the volume the instant status of a classic: it is a weighty tome, a book for individuals' libraries, a collection perhaps to be owned rather than read and few surviving copies show traces of early readers. It was also expensive, probably not less than 15*s*. a copy and often costing £1 or more. It remained expensive, with copies in the early twentieth century selling for over $50,000 and one being sold in October 2001 for over $6 million, six times the previous record price for a copy. The first folio's status as a library book probably helped so many copies to survive: over 220 are known, nearly eighty of them in the Folger Shakespeare Library in Washington.

In addition to the plays, preface, portrait, and dedication, the volume included a list of the principal actors in the plays and three prefatory poems, as well as Jonson's two, by Hugh Holland, Leonard Digges, and I. M. (probably James Mabbe). It amounts to a grand but not excessively elaborate quantity of prefatory material.

Without the first folio it is likely that most of the eighteen plays printed there for the first time would never have been printed at all. In effect, half Shakespeare's reputation rests on that publication. No literary volume has generated so much commentary and analysis. Technical study of its printing means that more is known about the processes of its production than for any other early modern book. There have been numerous facsimiles and, of course, innumerable reprintings of its contents.

The volume was first announced in October 1622—prematurely, for copies were not on sale for more than a year. William Jaggard was dead by November 1623 and it is his son's name that appears on the title-page. The first known purchase of a copy, by Sir Edward Dering, was in December 1623. Sales were brisk enough to warrant the printing of a second edition in 1632, with three more prefatory poems, including John Milton's first published poem, and with careful revision of the plays to correct many errors (and introduce some more). The quality of the paper led the scourge of the players, William Prynne, to complain that 'Shackspeers Plaies are printed in the best Crowne paper, far better than most Bibles' (W. Prynne, *Histriomastix*, 1633, sig. **6*v*). The third folio was published in 1663; a second issue in 1664 added seven more plays, only one of which, *Pericles*, is Shakespeare's while the others (including *The London Prodigal* and *Locrine*) belong to the body of Shakespeare apocrypha, keeping their place in the succession of Shakespeare editions for many years. A fourth folio was printed in 1685 and pages from it were reset to produce a putative 'fifth folio' probably shortly after 1700.

70 Publication of the poems was markedly less successful. Though *Venus and Adonis* and *The Rape of Lucrece* were frequently published up to the 1630s (at least fifteen and eight times respectively), each was printed only once more before 1700. The *Sonnets* were reprinted by John Benson in 1640 in an unauthorized version which ran a number of sonnets together to form longer works, gave many trivial titles (such as 'Love's relief' or 'The picture of true love'), and altered a few pronouns to reduce the emphasis on homoerotic desire. Benson also included many poems not by Shakespeare at all.

7

Becoming a classic

Performances and influences to 1660

Shakespeare's plays continued to be performed through the years before the theatres were closed in 1642. There were performances at the Globe and the Blackfriars but the casts were changing. As actors died or left the King's Men others took over their roles, but some thought it could not be the same: an elegy on the death of Richard Burbage in 1619 mourned:

> Kind Leer, the greved Moore, and more beside,
> That lived in him, have now for ever dy'de.
> (E. K. Chambers, *The Elizabethan Stage*, 1923, 2.309)

There were performances elsewhere: Sir Edward Dering's library contained an adaptation of the two parts of *Henry IV* into a single play, probably for a private performance. Some characters were already dominating their plays: a court performance of *1 Henry IV* on 1 January 1625 was referred to as *Sir John Falstaff*. But a remarkable range of plays which were hardly of the newest fashion were performed at Charles I's court, including *Othello*, *Hamlet*, *Julius Caesar*, *Cymbeline*, and *Richard III*. Charles himself was keen enough on Shakespeare to annotate his copy of the second folio, retitling *Much Ado* as 'Beatrice and Benedict'.

One other admirer at court was Sir William Davenant, whose ode on Shakespeare was published in 1638, the year he became poet laureate. Davenant, whose parents kept an inn in Oxford, variously claimed to be Shakespeare's godson and natural son, the latter especially when drunk.

More ambivalent, inevitably, were the responses of John Milton, who saw his happy man in 'L'Allegro' (*c*.1631), a poem full of Shakespeare echoes, going to the theatre to hear:

> sweetest Shakespeare, fancy's child,
> Warble his native wood-notes wild
> (ll. 133–4)

and whose *Comus* (1634) is pervasively influenced by Shakespeare. But if Shakespeare's work is never far from Milton's mind, especially in *Samson Agonistes* and *Paradise Lost*, his plays also stand, in Milton's prose writing, as tools with which to beat the crown: in *Eikonoklastes* (1649), Charles I is compared with Shakespeare's Richard III.

During the closure of the theatres in the interregnum and probably also in the early years of the Restoration, comic parts of Shakespeare's plays were performed for popular audiences as drolls at fairs, taverns, at the otherwise empty theatres, and elsewhere: versions of the gravedigger scene in *Hamlet* and the Gadshill robbery in *1 Henry IV* were printed in 1662 with a frontispiece showing Falstaff and Mistress Quickly, the first published illustration of Shakespearian characters, while the preface to *The Merry Conceited Humours of Bottom the Weaver* (1661), a very short version of *A Midsummer Night's Dream*, reported performances by apprentices.

Shakespeare adapted

When public performances resumed in 1660, Shakespeare was quickly put back into the repertory. The company playing at the Red Bull Theatre in late 1660 performed *Henry IV*, *The Merry Wives of Windsor* (another mark of the especial popularity of Falstaff), and *Othello*, while *Pericles* was at the Cockpit Theatre in Drury Lane. After November 1660 (when the two theatre companies under Thomas Killigrew and Sir William Davenant began competing operations) Killigrew's King's Company, claiming to be the successors to the King's Men, also claimed the rights in their predecessor's repertory, including Shakespeare.

On 11 December 1660 they performed *Othello* with one notable change: a woman played Desdemona. A new prologue 'to introduce the first Woman that came to Act on the Stage' noted the necessity:

> For (to speak truth) men act, that are between
> Forty and fifty, Wenches of fifteen;
> With bone so large, and nerve so incomplyant,
> When you call *Desdemona*, enter Giant.
> (T. Jordan, *A Royal Arbor of Loyal Poesie*, 1663, 21–2)

The next day, 12 December 1660, Davenant was awarded rights in nine Shakespeare plays (including *King Lear*, *Macbeth*, and *Hamlet*), following his proposition 'of reformeinge some of the most ancient Playes that were playd at Blackfriers and of makeinge them, fitt, for the Company of Actors appointed under his direction and Command' (A. Nicoll, *A History of*

English Drama, 1660–1900, 6 vols., 1952, 1.352). It is difficult to know which of the two changes was the more important. The replacement of the boy-actresses with women irrevocably changed the forms of Shakespearian representation. The right to alter plays seen as 'ancient' began the long history of Shakespeare adaptation. Each change had immense impact on Shakespeare in the theatre. A third major change was introduced in June 1661 when Davenant's company moved to the Lincoln's Inn Fields Theatre which was equipped with moveable scenery, the first ever in England. Not everyone was impressed: Richard Flecknoe wrote in 1664 'that which makes our Stage the better, makes our Playes the worse perhaps, they striving now to make them more for sight, then hearing' (R. Flecknoe, *Love's Kingdom*, 1664, sig. G7*v*).

Shakespeare's plays were not especially popular at this time and his name was not one yet able to draw the crowds. Davenant made *Henry VIII* a success in 1663 by spectacular new scenery and costumes and the performance of Thomas Betterton as Henry was exceptional, not least through being part of a tradition: 'he being Instructed in it by Sir *William* [Davenant], who had it from Old Mr. *Lowen*, that had his Instructions from Mr. *Shakespear* himself' (J. Downes, *Roscius Anglicanus*, 1709, 24). Samuel Pepys was regularly impressed by the new scenery and especially by Betterton's acting in Shakespeare, praising his Hamlet as 'beyond imagination' in August 1661 (E. L. Avery and others, *The London Stage, 1660–1700*, 1965, 32). Others were less excited: John Evelyn who saw the production in December 1661 thought that 'now the old playe began to disgust this refined age' (ibid., 43).

Pepys, who often saw Shakespeare plays among his many theatre visits, seeing *Macbeth* and *The Tempest* especially frequently, offers some sense of how a member of the audience estimated Shakespeare's worth. Some plays he admired; others disappointed. *A Midsummer Night's Dream* was 'the most insipid ridiculous play that ever I saw in my life' but relieved by 'some good dancing and some handsome women' (E. L. Avery and others, *The London Stage, 1660–1700*, 1965, 56). Both qualities mattered to Pepys. While he respected *Macbeth* as 'a deep tragedy', he particularly enjoyed the 'variety of dancing and music' (ibid., 100, 107). After his first visit to *The Tempest* he praised a musical echo effect and later noted that the play was 'full of so good variety, that I cannot be more pleased almost in a comedy' (ibid., 123).

In neither case was Pepys seeing Shakespeare's play unaltered. Davenant's *Macbeth* substantially added to the spectacle of the witches' scenes; Downes noted that:

> being drest in all it's Finery, as new Cloath's, new Scenes, Machines, as flyings for the Witches; with all the Singing and Dancing in it ... it being all Excellently perform'd, being in the nature of an Opera, it Recompenc'd double the Expence. (J. Downes, *Roscius Anglicanus*, 1709, 33)

Less play than opera (for its effects as much as its music), Davenant's version also increased the actresses' roles, emphasized Macbeth's ambition with a dying line 'Farewell vain World, and what's most vain in it, Ambition' ([W. Davenant], *Macbeth*, 1674, 60), and cleaned up the language: Macbeth no longer curses the 'cream-faced loon' asking 'Where gott'st thou that goose look?' (V. iii, ll. 11–12) but politely enquires 'Now Friend, what means thy change of Countenance?' (54). Such linguistic changes were necessary: Shakespeare's vocabulary was difficult, his syntax obscure, and his fascination with metaphor unacceptable since 'the tongue in general is so much refined since

 Shakespeare's time' as John Dryden noted in 1679 (J. Dryden, *Troilus and Cressida*, 1679, sig. A4*v*).

Davenant's adaptation of *Hamlet* makes similar changes, altering 'To grunt and sweat under a weary life' (III.i, l. 79) into 'To groan and sweat under a weary life', and 'the native hue of resolution' (III.i, l. 86) becomes 'the healthful face of resolution', no longer 'Sicklied o'er with the pale cast of thought' (III.i, l. 87) but now 'Shews sick and pale with thought' ([W. Davenant], *Hamlet*, 1676, 39). Davenant's playing text marked extensive cuts, according to the edition of 1676, in the places 'least prejudicial to the Plot or Sense' because the play was 'too long to be conveniently Acted'. But the edition also includes the full text 'that we may no way wrong the incomparable Author' (sig. [A]2*r*). Clearly, by this date, Shakespeare, simply an old dramatist at the Restoration, was becoming valued.

While Davenant's first Shakespeare adaptation, combining *Measure for Measure* and *Much Ado* into *The Law Against Lovers* (1662), was much more extreme, his version of *The Tempest* as *The Enchanted Island*, a collaboration with Dryden first produced in 1667, was a case of adding to the play's symmetry. Dryden's preface, which saw Fletcher's *The Sea-Voyage* (1622) and Sir John Suckling's *The Goblins* (1638) as earlier responses to the play, praised Davenant for contriving a 'Counterpart to *Shakespear*'s Plot' in balancing Miranda with Hippolito, 'a Man who had never seen a Woman' (Davenant and Dryden, *The Tempest*, 1670, sig. A2*v*). The new action with four lovers is by turns innocent and outrageously sexy. But much more striking is the expansion of the action of rebellion, with more sailors and a broader representation of the chaos of disorder. The adaptation manifests the deep cultural unease of a society only just recovering from civil war, making of Shakespeare's play, as with other early adaptations of pre-Restoration drama and with the new tragi-comedies being written, a fiercely political parable.

Other adaptations sought different solutions to making the plays stage-worthy again: James Howard wrote a happy ending for *Romeo and Juliet* in 1662 with the lovers left alive, the adaptation being played on alternate nights with the tragic original; John Lacy turned Grumio in *Shrew* into a Scot in his farcical adaptation *Sauny the Scot* (1667) in which he starred, with the play now set in London. The Dryden–Davenant *Tempest* was itself adapted by Thomas Shadwell in 1674 into a spectacular version with more machines, stage effects, and much more music, compensated for by cutting the text hard to make room. Howard's play is lost, *Sauny* was popular for a while, but Shadwell's *Tempest*, rescored by Purcell in 1690, lasted over a century. Like Davenant's *Macbeth*, the new version displaced Shakespeare's from the stage. Other plays could be used as, in effect, the raw material for theatrical spectacle, most notably the version of *A Midsummer Night's Dream* as *The Fairy Queen* (1692), again with music by Purcell, whose scenes do not set a single word by Shakespeare. The adaptations also became part of the wars between the theatres: the Duke's Company's success with Shadwell's *The Tempest* provoked the King's Company to put on Thomas Duffett's parody *The Mock-Tempest* (1674), the first in a long line of Shakespeare burlesques. Duffett also mocked the rival company's *Macbeth* in his farce on *The Empress of Morocco* (1674). In both cases it is not Shakespeare that is being mocked; his plays are the convenient vehicle for mocking rivals' theatrical styles.

Praising Shakespeare

None of this was incompatible with increasing praise for Shakespeare himself. Dryden, who became as crucial to the next phase of Shakespeare adaptation as Davenant had been at first, defined Shakespeare as the crucial originating natural force which enabled others:

> *Shakespear*, who (taught by none) did first impart
> To *Fletcher* Wit, to labouring *Johnson* Art.
> He Monarch-like gave those his subjects law,
> And is that Nature which they paint and draw.

Dryden here also identifies Shakespeare as the poetic equivalent of divine kingship: '*Shakespear*'s pow'r is sacred as a King's' (Davenant and Dryden, *The Tempest*, 1670, sig. A4*r*). The concepts of Shakespeare as natural genius and as a sacred king were both of immense and potent influence. Throughout his career Dryden sustainedly turns to Shakespeare as a measure of value. It is Shakespeare who is Dryden's example of the supreme dramatist in his *Essay of Dramatic Poesy* (1668), 'the man who of all Modern, and perhaps Ancient Poets, had the largest and most comprehensive soul' (J. Dryden, *Of Dramatick Poesie: an Essay*, 1668, 47). His own *All for Love* (1678) was an attempt 'to intimate the Divine *Shakespeare*' (sig. b4*v*). Even in his preface to his version of *Troilus and Cressida* (1679), a work about which he felt unsure, he identifies Shakespeare as being 'held in the same veneration . . . by us' as Aeschylus was by the Athenians (sig. A4*v*), while the prologue to the play is spoken by Shakespeare's ghost: 'See, my lov'd *Britons*, see your *Shakespeare* rise' (sig. b4*r*).

But Dryden's degree of praise was still unusual. It was shared by Margaret Cavendish, whose letter on Shakespeare was published in 1664 and ranks as the first lengthy critical assessment of his work. For her, Shakespeare's brilliant characterization would make one 'think he had been Transformed into every one of those Persons he hath Described', an early example of praise of Shakespeare for protean transformation (Thompson and Roberts, 12). Few went as far the other way as the critic Thomas Rymer, who in *A Short View of Tragedy* (1693) damned *Othello* as 'a Bloody Farce' (p. 146), mockingly suggesting that its morals were to advise 'all good Wives that they look well to their Linnen' and 'a lesson to Husbands, that before their Jealousie be Tragical, the proofs may be Mathematical' (p. 89).

Political Shakespeare

Nahum Tate was only stating a common view rather than an extreme one when he described *King Lear* as 'a Heap of Jewels, unstrung and unpolisht' (N. Tate, *King Lear*, 1681, sig. A2*v*). His concern to find an 'Expedient to rectifie what was wanting in the Regularity and Probability of the Tale' led to his writing in a love between Edgar and Cordelia and altering the ending to 'conclude in a Success to the innocent distrest Persons' (ibid., sigs. A2*v*–A3*r*). With no Fool to trouble the tragic tone and a new love scene for Edmund and Regan 'amorously Seated' in 'A Grotto' (ibid., 40), Tate's version (1681), the most notorious of the adaptations, may be designed to make the play more manageably moving but it is also a serious attempt to read the play politically, celebrating the king's 'blest Restauration' (ibid., 66). Equally political and topical was his attempt to stage *Richard II* in 1680, first banned outright and then, after two days of performances transposed to Italy as *The Sicilian Usurper*, banned again. Tate was not much luckier with his version of *Coriolanus* as *The Ingratitude of a Commonwealth* (1681), clearly establishment in its politics but not much liked by audiences.

As Tate found, amid the upheavals of the Popish Plot and the exclusion crisis, Shakespeare's plays were means of making dangerous political statements: Ravenscroft's *Titus Andronicus* (1678) was a satire on Titus Oates and the whigs; Otway's *Caius Marius* (1679), from *Romeo and Juliet*, explored the plight of those caught up in political and social struggles. Tate's problems with censorship were not the last: Colley Cibber's *Richard III* (1700), a version long-lived enough to leave traces on Laurence Olivier's film (1955), was first performed without its first act, borrowed from *3 Henry VI*, since the murder of a king was still unstageable when likely to be seen as a parallel to the death of James II. Cibber carefully distinguished his lines from Shakespeare's in the printed text, again a mark of Shakespeare's growing importance as an originating text.

Adaptations apart, the whole course of drama was being profoundly affected by Shakespeare. Playwrights creating Restoration comedies found their crucial prototypes for the wit-combats of hesitant lovers in Beatrice and Benedick while *Love's Labour's Lost* offered a model for a comedy that did not end with marriage but with future trials, a vital component in the work of George Etherege and others. Otway's fascination with Shakespearian tragedy led directly to his brand of pathetic drama: *The History and Fall of Caius Marius* (1680) is the first in a long line of versions of *Romeo and Juliet* to have Juliet (here Lavinia) wake just before Romeo (Otway's Marius Junior) dies, allowing for a last desperate love scene together. It was natural for Nicholas Rowe, writing emotionally affecting tragedies centred on the sufferings of women in Otway's wake, to announce on the title-page that *The Tragedy of Jane Shore* (1714) was 'written in Imitation of Shakespeare's Style', the same phrase that Dryden had used on the title-page of *All for Love*.

Eighteenth-century Shakespeare: England and overseas

8

Editions by Rowe, Pope, and Theobald

Nicholas Rowe's play was written after his most significant engagement with Shakespeare. In 1709 Jacob Tonson published a six-volume edition of Shakespeare edited by Rowe, the first major attempt to re-edit Shakespeare since the first folio. Tonson had acquired shares in the copyright of many Shakespeare plays in 1707 as part of his self-definition as the pre-eminent publisher of the major works of English literature. The copyright remained with the firm until 1767 and the line of Shakespeare editions it published were reworkings and remarketings of the firm's property. In 1709 Shakespeare was the first in a series of English dramatists—followed by Congreve, Beaumont and Fletcher, Otway, Southerne, and Dryden. Tonson chose Rowe as editor, presumably because an eminent dramatist was the appropriately sympathetic figure to edit the plays.

Rowe modernized Shakespeare's spelling and punctuation, continuing a process begun in the later folios. But he was not a Shakespeare editor in a modern sense: though he knew there were textual problems with lines and scenes absent from the fourth folio (his copy-text) and needing to be supplied, he made such 'corrections' only in a fairly haphazard way, for example by printing the prologue to *Romeo and Juliet*, found in a quarto, at the end of the play. He emended some clear errors introduced by compositors, and one or two that he perceived as Shakespeare's own (in *Troilus*, for example, the anachronistic reference to 'Aristotle' (II.ii, l. 165) was altered to 'graver Sages'). More significantly, Rowe supplied lists of characters and regularized all the plays into five acts, completing a process begun in the first folio and entirely absent from the quartos. For some he also included scene divisions.

Rowe also added a number of scene locators, identifying where the play was set, often at the head of each scene. Many locations he borrowed from contemporary adaptations, so that Shakespeare's plays now appeared as if they were contemporary dramas. Rowe's locations cast a long shadow: Shakespeare's Lear is never out on a heath; Rowe borrowed the placing from Tate's version.

Although less elaborate than other Tonson editions, Rowe's Shakespeare was presented with illustrations, one per play, often derived from contemporary stagings, the first images to appear in print for most of the plays. Rowe also wrote the first substantial Shakespeare biography, 'Some account of the life', prefixed to the first volume, based on a few facts, more legends, and some material that Thomas Betterton had gathered in his 'Veneration for the memory of *Shakespear*' (*Works*, ed. Rowe, 1.xxxiv). Rowe's Shakespeare is a gentleman like Rowe himself, while his friends in retirement are other 'Gentlemen of the Neighbourhood' (ibid., xxxvi). Rowe's decision to include this short biography was based on his recognition that biographical curiosity is 'very Natural' and 'may sometimes conduce to the better understanding' of an author, even if Shakespeare's works 'may seem to many not to want a Comment' (ibid., ii). The hesitancy over the usefulness of a biography of Shakespeare for understanding the plays would be repeated many times in subsequent centuries.

Tonson retained the extra apocryphal plays added to the third folio but he excluded the poems. They were printed in an extra volume by a rival publisher, Edmund Curll, formatted to match Tonson's plays and edited by Charles Gildon partly from Benson's 1640 text. Gildon also contributed by far the longest critical account of Shakespeare's plays yet to have appeared, carefully evaluating Shakespeare by classical precepts and assuming his pre-eminence among English dramatists.

In the subsequent years the pile of editions and of critical writings on Shakespeare began to grow apace. John Dennis's *Essay upon the Genius and Writings of Shakespeare* (1712), probably the first critical work devoted entirely to Shakespeare, was an extension of his other writing on Shakespeare and his experience as an unsuccessful adapter of *The Merry Wives of Windsor*. Shakespeare was discussed more often than any other literary figure in Richard Steele's periodical *The Tatler*, his finest passages identified and praised, his works harnessed to the defence of English writing against French, his plays alluded to and assumed to be known to Steele's readership.

Rowe revised his edition in 1714 but the whole text was re-edited by Alexander Pope and published in 1725. Pope undertook rather more careful collation of different texts, but his concern was to make contemporary readers appreciate the best passages, marking them with marginal quotation marks and providing a convenient index to them. This fragmenting of the dramas into convenient poetical passages continued in the excerpting of Shakespeare in William Dodd's *The Beauties of Shakespeare* (1752), a lasting anthology that for many, including Goethe, provided an introduction to Shakespeare. Pope also relegated to the foot of the page any passages he decided were weak, especially Shakespeare's increasingly unacceptable puns and conceits. For Pope, Shakespeare was 'the fairest and fullest subject for Criticism, and to afford the most numerous, as well as most conspicuous instances, both of Beauties and Faults of all sorts' (*The Works of Shakespear*, ed. A. Pope, 6 vols., 1725, 1.i). The plays could be regarded as 'an ancient majestick piece of *Gothick* Architecture, compar'd with a neat Modern building' (ibid., xxiii).

While Pope could consult twenty-seven texts for his edition, a sign of the growing libraries of Shakespeare which individuals were beginning to accumulate, Lewis Theobald listed forty-three. Theobald, who had attacked the defects of Pope's edition in *Shakespeare Restored* (1726), published his own in 1733, bringing to Shakespeare the methods of classical and biblical editorial theory and commentary. Careful collation and judicious emendation needed, for Theobald, considerable intellectual skill, though his mockery of Pope's failings only immortalized him as the hero of *The Dunciad* (1728). Theobald also published *The Double Falsehood*, his stage adaptation of what he claimed to be the Shakespeare–Fletcher 'Cardenio'.

The age of Johnson and Malone

More editions followed: Hanmer's opulent one published in Oxford in 1744, Warburton's wilful version for the Tonsons in 1747, Dr Johnson's thoughtful account first outlined in his

Proposals (1756) and adumbrated throughout his edition (1765) with its preface attempting to defend Shakespeare's generic hybrids against neo-classical orthodoxies. For Johnson, it is Shakespeare's depiction of 'general nature' that overrides local breaches of decorum and Shakespeare, 'the poet of nature', is more vital and more human, showing 'human sentiments in human language' (S. Johnson, *Preface to his Edition of Shakespear's Plays*, 1765, viii, xii). Johnson may blame Shakespeare for his faults, especially his fascination with puns ('the fatal Cleopatra', ibid., xxiii–xxiv), and he may find the tragedies at times laboured, resulting in 'meanness, tediousness and obscurity' (ibid., xxi), but for Johnson Shakespeare is the central figure in British culture and language, as the enormous number of citations in Johnson's *Dictionary* shows.

Other kinds of Shakespeare criticism also started to appear: Charlotte Lennox brought together many of Shakespeare's sources with a commentary in *Shakespeare Illustrated* (1753–4); Lord Kames made Shakespeare the example of genius as part of his exploration of moral aesthetics in *Elements of Criticism* (1762); Richard Farmer offered careful consideration of Shakespeare's classical learning (1767); Elizabeth Griffith explored *The Morality of Shakespeare's Drama* (1775); Maurice Morgann's *Essay on the Dramatic Character of Sir John Falstaff* (1777) turned from the nature of a single character, widely admired as Shakespeare's crowning achievement, to the nature of Shakespeare's art; Samuel Ayscough's *Index* (1790) was the first reasonably systematic concordance to Shakespeare. Cumulatively it adds up to the development of a critical industry focused on Shakespeare, making his work both a centre of attention and a means of evaluating other concerns, whether moral, aesthetic, or theoretical. But it also defines a literary culture within which the recognition and just evaluation of

Shakespeare's worth was increasingly seen as a central emblem of the culture's refinement and taste.

All was, however, still based on the achievements of successive editors. George Steevens reprinted a group of quartos in their original spelling in 1766. Edward Capell was the first to resist the random attempts of his predecessors by an assiduous and accurate collation of early texts, coupled with cautious emendation, resulting in a finely printed text (published in 1768) with brief textual notes. Capell's modesty contrasted with the increasing grandeur of the editions, building on Johnson's, which Steevens published in 1773 and subsequently expanded, with increasingly lengthy introductions, the text vanishing beneath the accumulated notes of editors and the whole a colossal display of the editors' learning.

Edmond Malone's immense achievement was the discovery of numerous records of Shakespeare's life, of the stage conditions of early modern theatres, and of textual materials, the synthesis of this vast archival research into new and remarkable accounts of the chronology of Shakespeare's plays (first published in 1780) and of Shakespeare's biography, and the application in his editing of a scrupulous textual analysis. This was most visible in his ten-volume edition of 1790, the first to include the poems, which was expanded into twenty-one volumes by James Boswell in 1821. Malone's work is the culmination of eighteenth-century editing and the foundation for all subsequent editing to the present, an extraordinary scholarly success. But it is also the sign of the literary icon and library figure that Shakespeare, in this major thread in his afterlife, had become.

By contrast with such scholarship, there was another strand of new editions reflecting performance. Adaptations continued to be written and printed but the theatrical texts, the versions of the plays that were being used with comparatively little adaptation, were also being published. In 1773–4 John Bell printed the first complete works to represent the acting editions 'Regulated from the Prompt Books of each House'. The introductions and commentary by Francis Gentleman identify the theatres' cuts (to deal with the problem of length) and the embarrassing indecencies—aspects of the plays which scholarly editing could play down, but which were glaringly visible in public performance. Later printings by Bell included a number of illustrations, strikingly unlike the fictional scenes in Theobald's or Hanmer's editions, now showing the characters by imaging the actors and actresses who played them.

Garrick's Shakespeare

The icon that scholarly editors celebrated had himself become increasingly visible elsewhere. In 1735 a bust of Shakespeare was included in the new Temple of British Worthies in Viscount Cobham's garden at Stowe. Money was raised by benefit performances of *Julius Caesar* and *Hamlet* for a more important project: the erection of a statue of Shakespeare in Poets' Corner in Westminster Abbey. Peter Scheemakers's statue, showing Shakespeare leaning on a plinth, was unveiled in 1741. The blank sheet to which Shakespeare was pointing was much mocked and later filled with a misquotation from *The Tempest*. Frequently reproduced, including in the late twentieth century on £20 notes, the statue also appeared on stage in 1741, discovered at the end of *Harlequin Student* at Goodman's Fields Theatre, the untheatrical monument now appropriated for performance. At one performance, the Harlequin in the play was performed by David Garrick.

Nothing that happened in Shakespeare performance in the first half of the eighteenth century quite anticipated the effect of Garrick's arrival. Many Shakespeare plays were established as the backbone of the theatrical repertory: by 1740 nearly a quarter of all London performances were of Shakespeare. There were great actors: for instance, Robert Wilks as Hamlet, Barton Booth as Othello, or James Quin as Falstaff. There was the advocacy of the Shakespeare Ladies' Club which from 1736 successfully pressed for the restoration of more of Shakespeare's plays to the stage. The elevation of Shakespeare to the embodiment of nation meant that adaptation became increasingly seen as unpatriotic: as William Guthrie wondered in 1747, 'Where is the Briton so much a Frenchman to prefer the highest stretch of modern improvement to the meanest spark of Shakespeare's genius?' (W. Guthrie, *An Essay upon English Tragedy*, 1747, 10).

Although many adaptations were still performed, the comedies, in particular, began to be played unadapted and admired: Charles Macklin's Shylock was praised, perhaps by Alexander Pope, as 'This is the Jew / That Shakespeare drew' (Bate and Jackson, 66) because, not least, it was Shakespeare's Shylock, not that of Lansdowne's 1701 adaptation, and Macklin played the role from 1740 to 1789.

But Garrick's triumph as Richard III in 1741 changed much. Painted by William Hogarth, one of the growing number of paintings which now sought to represent Shakespeare in performance, Garrick's Richard startled through its power and modernity. Garrick, the most frequently painted figure of the century, was often portrayed in Shakespearian roles in great works by Zoffany, Fuseli, Wilson, and others, adding to the expanding store of visual images of Shakespeare. Throughout his long career, Garrick sought to put more and more of Shakespeare's text back into performance, even while adapting it; his version of *Hamlet* in 1772 was reviled for eliminating almost all of act V but the cuts left space to restore much elsewhere. Shakespeare was, as Garrick wrote, borrowing from *Romeo*, 'the god of my idolatry' (Bate and Jackson, 71), a divinity emphasized by his erection of a temple in the garden of his villa on the Thames with a statue by Roubiliac. On Garrick's death the statue was bequeathed to the British Museum and now stands at the entrance of the British Library. Garrick also left to the museum his large collection of plays, a resource which he freely lent to Capell, Steevens, and other Shakespeare scholars.

Garrick's advocacy of Shakespeare was not always triumphant: his adaptation of *A Midsummer Night's Dream* with George Colman was a failure in 1763 and he was unable to restore the tragic ending of *King Lear*. Other adaptations, especially his *Catherine and Petruchio* (from *Shrew*) and *Florizel and Perdita* (from *The Winter's Tale*), performed as a double bill in 1756, fared better. His Romeo was less passionate than Spranger Barry's, performed at Covent Garden head to head with Garrick's at Drury Lane in 1748, but Garrick's adaptation with its grand funeral scene for Juliet and dying reunion of the lovers was a lasting success. In every role Garrick was minutely examined by the audience; the high points of his performances, especially as Hamlet, Macbeth, and Lear, were seen as overwhelming in the force and range of the emotions he explored. Garrick's dominance was also Shakespeare's and the two were as intertwined in the culture as in the lines on Garrick's Westminster Abbey monument, 'Shakespeare and Garrick like twin stars shall shine', or the comment in a 1752 pamphlet, 'Shakespeare revives! In Garrick breathes again!' (Dobson, 168).

Garrick's most expensive and vulnerable act of homage to Shakespeare was the Stratford jubilee of 1769, his response to Stratford upon Avon's flattery. The event lasted three days, including a masked ball, fireworks, concerts, processions, and a horse race. There was no performance of a Shakespeare play, only of Thomas Arne's sacred oratorio *Judith*. The crowning event was Garrick's ode; answering a planted heckling speech complaining that Shakespeare was a provincial nobody, it spoke of Shakespeare's immortality and national significance, his exploration of nature, and his local roots. The success of the ode, which praised Shakespeare as 'The bard of all bards', in combination with Garrick's use in it of the phrase 'The god of our idolatry' from *Romeo*, did much to establish, if not to create, the notion of Shakespeare as a bard to be worshipped by bardolators.

Although rain washed out much of the celebrations, Garrick recouped his losses by staging his brief play *The Jubilee* at Drury Lane the next season, ending with a long procession of nineteen groups of Shakespeare's characters and a copy of the Shakespeare statue. Garrick's jubilee transformed the social significance of Stratford, putting the quiet town on the national map as Shakespeare's home. Its veneration of Shakespeare emblematized the semi-divine status Shakespeare now occupied. It also helped Garrick's own reputation considerably.

Widening horizons: continental appreciation and domestic forgery

While much of the emphasis on Shakespeare's importance was, throughout the eighteenth century, based on his image as virile symbol of the nation, Garrick had tried to persuade French friends to admire the plays. The history of Shakespeare performance outside England starts surprisingly early, with performances of *Hamlet* and *Richard II* in 1607 and 1608 on a ship becalmed off Sierra Leone for an audience of the ship's company and, for *Hamlet*, four African spectators. The performances were permitted, wrote Captain Keeling, 'to keep my people from idleness and unlawful games, or sleep' (I. Kamps and J. G. Singh, *Travel Knowledge*, 2001, 220).

Troupes of English actors touring central Europe (especially Germany and Poland) in the seventeenth century performed short plays, some of which were based on Shakespeare. Initially performing in English, the companies began to include local actors and perform in German. One group performed a *Hamlet* play in Dresden in 1626, though possibly not Shakespeare's. By the later seventeenth century a German company was playing a version of *Hamlet* called *Der bestrafte Brudermord* ('Fratricide punished'), about one-fifth the length of Shakespeare's, with the complexities of action, language, and thought ironed flat into a linear, exciting, and conventionally moral drama. There were versions of *Titus Andronicus* (published in German in 1620), *A Midsummer Night's Dream* (written *c*.1657), *The Merchant of Venice* (perhaps as early as 1611), and others. The English comedians had a profound effect on German theatre, in some respects creating a theatre culture where there had been none, and their repertory influenced the development of a vernacular drama.

In the eighteenth century German translations began to appear. The first, *Julius Caesar* in alexandrines by von Borck in 1741, prompted Lessing's defence of Shakespeare's compatibility with neo-classicism. Lessing's importance led to something approaching a German cult of Shakespeare, aided by Christoph Wieland's prose translations of twenty-two plays (1762–6). Wieland also put on *The Tempest* in Biberach in 1761, the first German production of an 'original' Shakespeare play. Shakespeare rapidly became a rallying cry for avant-garde writers: Herder's praise affected the young Goethe and Schiller, both of whom wrote early plays which were distinctly Shakespearian in ambition. In 1771 Goethe's speech 'On Shakespeare's day', at a domestic version of Garrick's jubilee, eloquently praised Shakespeare.

In Hamburg in 1776, where Lichtenberg's excited descriptions of Garrick's acting in Shakespeare had been published, Friedrich Schröder produced and starred in *Hamlet*, the first of ten Shakespeare plays staged there by 1780, with his *King Lear*, closer to Shakespeare than Tate's, particularly admired. Germany's obsession with *Hamlet* reached one climax in Goethe's *Wilhelm Meister's Apprenticeship* (1795–6), a novel dominated by the play and whose hero performs the role.

In France the process was more complex. Voltaire saw Shakespeare plays performed in England in the late 1720s, translated parts of *Hamlet* (printed 1733), and praised Shakespeare's 'monstrous farces' as signs of his 'genius full of ... naturalness, and sublimity, without the least spark of good taste and without the slightest knowledge of the rules' (J. Jusserand, *Shakespeare in France under the Ancien Régime*, 1899, 208). His own plays were based closely on Shakespearian models. But later in life he condemned Shakespeare outright, especially *Hamlet* which was, as Arthur Murphy translated it in 1753 while trying to defend Shakespeare against Voltaire's onslaught, 'a barbarous piece, abounding with such gross absurdities that it would not be tolerated by the vulgar of *France* and Italy' (Vickers, 4.91).

Some scenes from *Hamlet* were published by Pierre-Antoine de la Place in 1746 and a complete translation of the plays by Pierre Le Tourneur appeared in 1776–82. But the plays were slower to reach the stage, though Jean-François Ducis's neo-classical adaptations of *Hamlet* and five others between 1769 and 1792 were all performed at the Comédie-Française.

In Russia there were versions of *Hamlet* (by Sumarokov, 1750), of *Merry Wives* (by Catherine the Great, 1786), and a translation of *Julius Caesar* (by Karamzin, 1787). There was an Italian *Julius Caesar* published in 1756 and a version there of Ducis's *Hamlet* performed in 1774, while a Spanish version was staged in 1772. King Stanislaus of Poland translated *Caesar* into French, while a Czech *Macbeth* was staged in 1786. By the end of the eighteenth century Shakespeare was being translated and performed, praised and attacked across almost the whole of Europe. Whatever ambivalent responses his plays provoked, they could not be ignored.

In England, too, by this point, Shakespeare's plays were part of the common currency of the culture. Alderman Boydell set up his Shakspeare Gallery in 1789 with scenes from Shakespeare painted by Barry, Fuseli, Northcote, Reynolds, Romney, and others. Boydell was concerned both to expand his print business and to establish a new school of English history painting, combining commerce with cultural and national aspirations. Mocked by many, the gallery was auctioned off in 1805. Its most brilliant critic was the caricaturist James Gillray, whose political cartoons frequently use witty and complex allusions to lines from Shakespeare to make his satiric points, another mark of the extent to which Shakespeare's language had penetrated deep into the culture.

Shakespearian documents were also valuable enough in both cultural and financial terms to be worth forging. In 1795–6 William Henry Ireland forged poems and letters, legal deeds and receipts, all supposedly written or signed by Shakespeare. He forged manuscripts for *Hamlet* and *King Lear* and three complete and hitherto unknown plays, *Vortigern* (later staged for one night by Sheridan to howls of derision from the audience), *Henry II*, and *William the Conqueror*. Ireland's father, Samuel, opened his house to display these relics and James Boswell, wholly convinced, knelt before them, giving 'thanks to God that I have lived to see them' (Schoenbaum, *Records*, 129). In 1796 Edmond Malone exposed the forgeries by careful scholarship and William Henry Ireland confessed in print a few years later, though his father died still believing the documents were genuine.

9 Romantic Shakespeare

Shakespeare and English Romanticism

English Romanticism produced its own particular, immensely powerful and influential versions of Shakespeare. At its greatest, in the criticism of Hazlitt and Coleridge or in the poetry of Keats and Wordsworth, Shelley and Byron, and at its weakest, in their plays, Shakespeare became the touchstone for a new kind of writing, the original genius who embodied the natural rather than the educated, the denier of conventions rather than their slave, the creator of a whole world of characters whose individual consciousnesses explored the full extent of the human mind. As painters found in Shakespeare possibilities of the imagination with little connection to drama or theatre, so poets saw the plays as poems of the mind, spaces of thought and feeling with a kind of power that was unequalled. In 1811 Charles Lamb argued that *King Lear* should not be staged, not only because of the adapters' changes but also because 'while we read it, we see not Lear, but we are Lear,—we are in his mind' (Bate, *Romantics*, 123); for Lamb, reading allowed emotions of delight and terror that staging never could.

Significantly, while continuing the previous generations' praise of *Hamlet*, the poets raised *King Lear* to a new position of accomplishment, Hazlitt, Coleridge, and Shelley explicitly identifying it as Shakespeare's greatest achievement. It was also a play that could be engaged with only in reading, for performances were still of versions derived from Nahum Tate. Hazlitt's praise of what he saw as Shakespeare's sympathy with all his characters affected Keats (who heard Hazlitt lecture), who developed his own theory of Shakespeare's 'negative capability'; this was a chameleon quality in which Shakespeare became the ideal of that protean creator with no identity of his own that Keats aspired to be. Coleridge's poetry was the proof of the admiration for Shakespeare he later expressed in his criticism, which survives only in the form of random comments and reports of his lectures. Brilliant in its perception (for instance in his description of one of Iago's soliloquies as 'the motive-hunting of a motiveless malignity'; Bate, *Romantics*, 485) and with a continually startling originality, Coleridge's criticism shows the depth of a great poet's engagement with the complexity of Shakespeare.

All the Romantic poets found themselves, whether they wished or not, deeply influenced by Shakespeare, endlessly alluding to his plays as the ultimate poetic authority for their own writing, defining Shakespeare's genius as their crucial forerunner. If Wordsworth was prepared to criticize Shakespeare, he also embedded him into his attempts at drama like *The Borderers* (1796–7) and in the quotations and references found throughout *The Prelude* and in the rest of his work. It was a conflict of public rejection and poetic acceptance that was also to be pervasively characteristic of Byron who, even as he mockingly rejected Shakespeare as 'the *worst* of models', praised him as 'the most extraordinary of writers' (*Byron's Letters and*

Journals, ed. L. Marchand, 12 vols., 1973–82, 8.152). Byron's comedy in *Don Juan*, as much as his tragedy in plays like *Manfred*, is profoundly and openly indebted to Shakespeare, whose work pervades every aspect of Byron's writing.

If English Romanticism's responses to Shakespeare were not primarily directed at the stage, they were responsive to it. Late eighteenth-century Shakespeare theatre production was dominated by John Philip Kemble and his sister Sarah Siddons. Her awesome power as Lady Macbeth, especially in the sleepwalking scene, and as Queen Katherine in *Henry VIII* astonished, terrified, and moved audiences. Her preparation for the former, copying a sleepwalker she had seen and trying to find an imaginative sympathy with the character, fed her representation of a dark sublime.

Kemble was most praised for the nobility of his performances, for an aristocratic hauteur that was the essence of a high classical style—hence his success as Shakespeare's Roman heroes. His *Coriolanus*, his own adaptation that used Shakespeare heavily cut for the first three acts and then interwove Shakespeare's play with James Thomson's adaptation (1749), was emphatically in favour of the hero. As a political reading of the play—and Shakespeare was continually being co-opted into contemporary politics as authority and allusion, adaptation and interpretation allowed opposing appropriations of the plays—Kemble's *Coriolanus* disturbed Hazlitt whose liberal politics were at the other pole from this conservative reading. Shakespeare's play, placed in the intersection of theatre, criticism, and contemporary political events, became the site across which politics could be contested.

When Kemble rebuilt Covent Garden Theatre after a fire and raised prices, the resulting riots in 1809 (which lasted sixty-seven nights and which ended only with Kemble's capitulation to the rioters' demands) were a matter of class and power, an argument that Shakespeare belonged to the whole nation, not solely to the aristocratic or the rich. The theatre itself became the place where the tensions of the society could be fully exposed, but Shakespeare as the national bard was the property that was being contested and through him the rights of citizens of that nation. This sense of Shakespeare's presence in the culture is typified, though from a perspective far from that of the rioters, by Henry Crawford's comments in Jane Austen's *Mansfield Park* (1814): 'But Shakespeare one gets acquainted with without knowing how. It is a part of an Englishman's constitution ... one is intimate with him by instinct.'

Against the traditional authority of Kemble were placed the productions of the illegitimate theatres. Their burlesques and travesties, like John Poole's *Hamlet Travestie* (New Theatre, 1811), were a continuation of the eighteenth century's use of Shakespeare as a resource for parody and mockery of contemporary theatre and politics. It was a rich tradition with wonderfully comic work by Charles Selby, Francis Talfourd, William and Robert Brough, and F. C. Burnand, stretching at least as far as W. S. Gilbert's *Rosencrantz and Guildenstern* (staged 1891). But the battle between the patent houses, Kemble's Covent Garden and the rival Drury Lane, was also fought out as a conflict of styles: Kemble's patrician classicism against the new style of Edmund Kean, who from his Drury Lane début in 1814 was the very embodiment of a radical, natural, and emotional force. Kean electrified audiences and destroyed Kemble's authority. Often drunk on stage, full of sexual energy (regularly having sex with a prostitute before and in the intervals of his performances), Kean could be bad as well as brilliant: Coleridge's praise of him as 'like reading Shakspeare [*sic*] by flashes of lightning' is not necessarily a compliment (Bate, *Romantics*, 160). But Kean's was the kind of acting that Romanticism sought.

European Romanticism

In the battles of European Romanticism, Shakespeare played a crucial part. August Wilhelm Schlegel's criticism was effective but it was his translation of the plays (1797–1810), later completed by Ludwig Tieck and Tieck's daughter Dorothea, which defined German responses to Shakespeare thereafter. The subtlety of the translations' attempts to capture form as well as meaning, their close links to the style of contemporary German drama, and the ways in which they extended the possibilities of German dramatic verse all made Shakespeare's plays central to German thought and poetry. German Romanticism appropriated Shakespeare and made him its own.

French Romanticism was, by contrast, directly influenced by the cross-channel movement of the theatre company of Charles Kemble, John Philip's brother. In 1823 in *Racine et Shakespeare* Stendhal defined Shakespeare as the vital source for a modern drama. In 1827 Victor Hugo argued in the preface to his play *Cromwell* that 'Shakespeare, c'est le Drame' ('Shakespeare *is* drama' quoted in Bate, *Genius*, 231). Hugo's commitment to Shakespeare underscores his play *Hernani*, whose première in 1830 was the battleground and triumph of French Romantic drama. His son, François-Victor, completed a prose translation of all Shakespeare's works in 1865 and Victor Hugo contributed a long preface, later published separately (in English, French, and German) for the tercentenary of Shakespeare's birth in 1864 and dedicated to England. Hugo's was for long the standard literary translation, though never used in production.

In 1827, the year of Hugo's *Cromwell*, Charles Kemble's company performed *Hamlet* in Paris to an audience which included all the major figures of the French Romantic movement. An extraordinary success, the production overwhelmed Dumas *père* (who wrote later 'I recognised at last that [Shakespeare] was the man who had created most after God'; *Théâtre complet*, 1863–5, 1.15), Eugène Delacroix (who created over the next thirty years a series of powerful lithographs of scenes from the play), and Berlioz (who would later marry Kemble's Ophelia, Harriet Smithson).

Shakespeare and nineteenth-century music and literature

Berlioz's greatest music was from then on often explicitly Shakespearian: from the 'Fantasy on *The Tempest*' in *Lélio* (op. 14b, 1830), his overture to *King Lear* (op. 4, 1831), and his dramatic symphony *Roméo et Juliette* (op. 17, 1839) to his quotations from *The Merchant of Venice* for the love scene in *Les Troyens* (1856–8) or the adaptation of *Much Ado about Nothing* as the opera *Béatrice et Bénédict* (1860–62).

If Berlioz is more completely a Shakespearian composer than any other, there was throughout the nineteenth century hardly a major composer who did not at some point write a Shakespeare-influenced piece: Mendelssohn's overture to *A Midsummer Night's Dream* was composed for the concert hall in 1826, with the rest of his incidental music written for the stage in 1843; Schubert wrote songs with Shakespeare texts in 1826; Liszt wrote his *Hamlet* symphonic poem first in 1858 (later revised); Tchaikovsky composed fantasy overtures to *Romeo and Juliet* (1869) and *Hamlet* (1888) and a fantasia on *The Tempest* (1873). Full-scale operas range from Salieri's *Falstaff* (1799) and Rossini's *Otello* (1816, revised 1819 with a happy ending) to Wagner's *Das Liebesverbot* (1836), from *Measure for Measure*, Nicolai's *Die lustigen Weiber von Windsor* (1849), and Ambroise Thomas's *Hamlet* (Paris, 1868). The three greatest nineteenth-century Shakespeare operas are Verdi's *Macbeth* (1847, revised 1865), *Otello* (1887), and *Falstaff* (1893), the last in its exuberance and intelligence fully equal to its source (and for some critics even greater than *Merry Wives*). There are also the fascinating unwritten projects like Mozart's *Tempest* and Verdi's *King Lear*. If initially Shakespeare is no more than a convenient source for a dramatic plot or a romantic mood, he comes to be the literary figure with whom composers must engage: Verdi's *Macbeth* has far less of an imaginative interaction with the full range of Shakespeare's text than his works forty and fifty years later.

Throughout Europe, writers, like composers, worked under the heavy influence, liberating and constricting by turns, of Shakespeare's presence. Shakespeare could enable new national forms of drama: in Russia, for instance, Pushkin's *Boris Godunov* (1825) used Shakespeare's characterization and his approach to historical drama as its model. He could make possible political attack: in Germany Freiligrath used Hamlet's indecision as the stick with which to beat the political pusillanimity of the German intelligentsia in his poem 'Germany is Hamlet' (1844), a reaction to the pro-*Hamlet* attitude after Goethe's celebration of the introspective hero. He could be the source for wholly new styles of writing: Horace Walpole's *The Castle of Otranto* (1765), the instigator of the Gothic novel, was explicit in its

 Shakespearian method and its mood (derived especially from *Macbeth* and *Hamlet*), as one of its successors, Lewis's *The Monk* (1796) depended on *Measure for Measure*; Sir Walter Scott's effective invention of the historical novel, starting with *Waverley* (1814), depended on a transformation of the range of concerns of Shakespeare's histories into narrative fiction, a metamorphosis sustained by frequent quotation and allusion. Scott could also fictionalize Shakespeare's life: in *Kenilworth* (1821) the chronology is so deliberately confused that in the age of Elizabeth people quote from Shakespeare's last plays, written a decade after the queen's death.

In England in particular, as for Walpole and Scott, the novel was the form in which the nineteenth century's imaginative engagements with Shakespeare were most powerfully present. Charlotte Brontë's *Shirley* (1849) deepens its analysis of industrial relations in the context of the Luddite riots in the Napoleonic era through a web of references to *Coriolanus*. For George Eliot, described as 'the female Shakespeare' (Taylor, 208), Shakespeare's writing was at times unacceptable (the ending of *Two Gentlemen of Verona* was impossible for her) and writing his biography was a task she turned down. But his work was also a means of defining her concerns all the more clearly. In *Daniel Deronda* (1876), for instance, the interplay between Gwendolen Harleth's re-creation of Rosalind in *As You Like It* and Deronda's *Hamlet*-influenced irresolution allows a tension between the plays to reflect the novel's antithesis of realism and Romanticism.

Charles Dickens, who knew Shakespeare as an actor and theatre critic as well as a reader, was unable to write a novel without extensive use of Shakespeare. Benign mockery of provincial Shakespeare production like Crummles's *Romeo and Juliet* in

Nicholas Nickleby (1839), a novel Dickens dedicated to the great actor–manager Macready, can be more troubling when Mr Wopsle performs *Hamlet* in *Great Expectations* (1861), a novel full of fathers missing, pretending, and returning. Every Dickens novel has a wealth of Shakespeare allusions and quotations, with characters and events demanding to be read against Shakespearian models, amounting in all to many hundreds of references. In some cases, a novel seems especially engaged with a particular play: *Dombey and Son* is permeated by references to *Macbeth*, both as a narrative of children and childlessness and as a drama of melodramatic murder.

Dickens's view of the world was focused through Shakespearian lenses. It is almost as if it is through Shakespeare's characters and action that Dickens saw, thought, and felt. But Shakespeare's presence also pervades much high Victorian poetry and painting, from Tennyson's 'Mariana' and Browning's 'Caliban upon Setebos' to the work of the pre-Raphaelites, Dante Gabriel Rossetti, Holman Hunt, and John Everett Millais.

Responses of the Victorian age

10

Lambs' *Tales* and new editions

Some attitudes to Shakespeare elsewhere in nineteenth-century society came from quite other needs. Shakespeare's plays required to be changed to make them accessible to children and acceptable for families. Charles and Mary Lamb produced their *Tales from Shakespeare* in 1807 (mostly written by Mary), turning the plays into placidly and even at times sentimentally moral stories that were also designed to free children's (and especially young girls') imaginations by their encounters with the worlds of the plays. Their versions have never been out of print since and have formed the first encounters with Shakespeare for many generations of children.

But if Shakespeare's plays themselves were to be part of family reading they needed censoring. The Lambs recommended that young boys should read passages from Shakespeare's 'manly book' to their sisters after 'carefully selecting what is proper for a young sister's ear' (Taylor, 207). Henrietta Bowdler's edition of twenty plays in 1807 'endeavoured to remove every thing that could give just offence to the religious and virtuous mind' to produce a text that could be given to boys and girls. *The Family*

Shakespeare was completed by her brother, the Revd Thomas Bowdler, in 1818. The cutting and rewritings produced plays that were safe. Both the Lambs' and the Bowdlers' work sold slowly at first but more successfully as the century continued and their values seemed appropriate.

Other kinds of edition were needed as well. The new technologies made cheap Shakespeare possible for nearly all: a complete Shakespeare could be sold for a shilling and other editions were published in penny issues. Shakespeare could become a part of everyone's library alongside the Bible (often the only two books in working-class homes). Other editions were more expensive but were attractive for their extensive illustrations. Charles Knight produced a long series of illustrated texts; his *Pictorial Shakespeare* (1838–41) sold in weekly parts before being available in bound volumes. Staunton's edition was first published at a shilling a play (1856–8) but there were 831 images by Sir John Gilbert. For the wealthy and for scholars, there could now be facsimiles of early texts: a photographic reproduction of the first folio was published in 1866 and the publication of photolitho quarto facsimiles began in 1858.

Scholars were also helped by the Globe Edition (1863–6), edited by William Clark, William Wright, and John Glover. Their work, the first to be edited by academics, became known as the Cambridge Shakespeare. Its significance lay not only in its careful collations (an extension of Malone's earlier work) and its reprinting of early quartos but also in its inclusion of line numbers, the first version to make referring to a particular line easy and accurate. Abbott's *A Shakespearian Grammar* (1869), Schmidt's *Shakespeare-Lexicon* (1874–5), and Bartlett's accurate complete concordance (1894) provided further important reference works for Shakespeare study. For Shakespeare was now being studied: from 1868 Clark and Wright edited a series of the plays for the Clarendon Press 'to meet the wants of Students in English Literature'; Abbott included questions to test students' understanding of the rules of grammar and prosody. A. W. Verity's Pitt Press Shakespeare (from 1893) and the Warwick Shakespeare served generations of schoolchildren through much of the twentieth century. As English literature emerged as a new and major subject for study at university, and schools also placed literature as a central requirement of children's education, so Shakespeare became the centre of an educational system both in Britain and across the British empire.

Shakespeare societies and the tercentenary, 1864

There were new ways of gathering to talk about Shakespeare, or to listen to lectures, or to preserve the Shakespeare heritage. The Shakespearian Club was founded in Stratford upon Avon in 1824, becoming the Royal Shakespeare Club from 1830 to 1874. Halliwell-Phillipps founded the scholarly Shakespeare Society in 1840 and Furnivall created its successor, the New Shakespeare Society, in 1873. The first major national Shakespeare society was the Deutsche Shakespeare-Gesellschaft, founded in 1864 and a sign of the immense importance of Shakespeare in Germany and of German Shakespeare scholarship to the growth of Shakespeare studies. Its journal *Shakespeare Jahrbuch* began publication in 1865.

The Royal Shakespeare Club had helped the campaign to purchase Shakespeare's birthplace as a national monument in 1847. The Shakespeare Birthplace Trust was formed soon afterwards, acquiring other houses over the years (for example, New Place and Nash's House in 1862, Anne Hathaway's Cottage in

1892)—Stratford had for some time been a place of pilgrimage, with John Keats and Walter Scott among the 700 a year visiting the birthplace and/or the grave. The visible material heritage of Shakespeare, redefined as houses associated with his family and his life rather than the theatres he wrote for or indeed the books he wrote, was now preserved for the world's visitors—and their piety superbly mocked by Henry James in his short story 'The Birthplace' (1903).

In 1864 the tercentenary of Shakespeare's birth was celebrated in a typically muddled English way. Perhaps the most public Shakespeare event of the century, it involved competing celebrations in Stratford and London, with two committees, the Stratford one dominated by Edward Fordham Flower whose family became central to Shakespeare in Stratford thereafter. The Stratford events, in spite of the piqued *amour propre* and late withdrawal of the actor Edward Fechter, went well: a banquet for thousands in the specially constructed pavilion, a fancy-dress ball, concerts, two Shakespeare sermons, and even, in contrast to Garrick's 1769 jubilee, performances of and readings from the plays. The National Shakespeare Committee tried chaotically to arrange London's contribution: a tree-planting ceremony on Primrose Hill was mixed up with a demonstration over Garibaldi and came close to a riot; a concert at Crystal Palace was more peaceable. More tangibly, the celebrations led in Stratford ultimately to the opening of the Shakespeare Memorial Theatre in 1879 and the memorial statues by Sir Ronald Gower of Shakespeare, Hamlet, Lady Macbeth, Prince Henry, and Falstaff that were unveiled in 1888.

The connection between the tercentenary tree planting and Garibaldi was not an accident. Instead, it demonstrates the centrality of Shakespeare to nineteenth-century radicalism. From the Chartists onwards, Shakespeare was a crucial part of radicals' literary culture. The few details of his life, with the absence of clear links to the court and his modest background, made him the perfect English exemplum of the ordinary man as poetic genius. His plays were widely used in political oratory, especially when cheap editions of them (like the *Complete Shilling Shakespeare* published by John Thomas Dicks in the 1850s) became available for working-class homes. Reformers read the plays as reformist documents, with his celebration of rural England seen as opposition to enclosures and other forms of dispossession of the rural poor. Shakespeare was identified as a scathing satirist of courts and kings, with plays like *Julius Caesar* co-opted as tracts against tyranny. Chartist newspapers could carefully document precursors to their own political demands throughout Shakespeare's works. Shakespeare became the people's playwright, with radicals fiercely opposing attempts either to appropriate his politics for Conservatism or to claim aristocrats as the true authors of the plays. In 1864 to celebrate Shakespeare and to demonstrate against the government's supposed expulsion of Garibaldi were naturally connected events for radical politics, part of the reclaiming of Shakespeare from the upper classes and their high culture as a different kind of national poet.

The authorship controversy

Within the century's enshrining of Shakespeare as the icon of the nation there were also other voices of opposition, especially the growth of the belief that the plays, acknowledged as masterpieces, could not possibly have been the work of the 'man from Stratford', a mere actor and not a poet (there are shades here of the Romantic glorification of the poet removed from the quotidian world). The idea that someone else had written the plays seems first to have been advanced by the Revd James Wilmot in 1785 (his candidate was Francis Bacon) but he destroyed his papers. In 1848 Joseph C. Hart, American consul at Santa Cruz, argued in *The Romance of Yachting* that the plays were written by university graduates and foisted off as Shakespeare's. In 1856 Delia Bacon claimed that Francis Bacon or a committee headed by him had been responsible. Her ascription was repeated, independently, by William Henry Smith the following year. Many editors from Pope onwards had doubted Shakespeare's responsibility for some speeches, scenes, even whole plays—but this was a dislodging of Shakespeare from any authorship of any of his work.

The controversy that followed was energetic. Other candidates emerged, including Edward de Vere, seventeenth earl of Oxford (proposed by J. Thomas Looney in 1920 and supported by Sigmund Freud), the earl of Rutland (the idea of Peter Alvor in Germany in 1906 and popular there for a while), the earl of Derby (first advanced in 1891 but most strongly in France after 1919), Christopher Marlowe (according to William Ziegler in 1895 and advanced even more strenuously by Calvin Hoffman in 1955), and Queen Elizabeth (George Elliott's proposal in 1956). All these claims surmount the contemporary evidence for Shakespeare by arguing for an early modern conspiracy and often a later one among academics and others to suppress the 'truth'. Many resolve the inconveniently early death of their candidate by arguing for posthumous slow release of the plays. Some indulge in cryptograms of mind-boggling complexity to reveal the hidden 'truth' of their assertions. Some, like Delia Bacon, were or became mad in pursuit of their claims. Marlowe apart, whose literary ability is unquestioned, all depend on assumptions that the plays display knowledge available only to an aristocrat, university educated, well travelled, and a habitué of courts. This snobbery is exemplified by the comment of Christmas Humphreys, an Oxfordian and a barrister, in 1955: 'It is offensive to scholarship, to our national dignity, and to our sense of fair play to worship the memory of a petty-minded tradesman' (Bate, *Genius*, 93). All distort evidence for their own ends. None is remotely convincing to scholars, though many others have been and remain steadfastly sure that Shakespeare could not have written Shakespeare.

Shakespeare in America and Russia

One of the striking things about the advocates of other authors is that many of the staunchest are Americans. Characterized by a nostalgia for an aristocracy lacking in their democracy and by their proneness to accept conspiracy theories, these anti-Stratfordians are part of the wide range of reactions to Shakespeare generated by Americans in the nineteenth century. By the end of the century there were a hundred Shakespeare societies in America, hardly a surprise in a country with at least four towns called Hamlet, three Othellos, three Romeos, two Violas, two Horatios, and an Iago. The ambivalence of the responses is an eloquent testimony to the interaction of writer and nation. For Ralph Waldo Emerson, who visited England in 1847, Shakespeare was the perfect poet for his list of *Representative Men* (1850), a genius whose works, half understood in his own time, were fully available only in modern America. Washington Irving's praise of Shakespeare in 1820 was set against his mockery of the Stratford tourist industry where Shakespeare's mulberry tree 'seems to have as extraordinary powers of self-multiplication as the wood of the true cross' (Rawlings, 43).

Some sought to make Shakespeare an honorary American, like Henry Cabot Lodge, who saw his language as close to current

American speech in 1895. Others were vehement that there is nothing unique or English about Shakespeare: Melville argued in 1850 that 'Shakespeares are this day being born on the banks of the Ohio' (Rawlings, 165). Still others, in seeking to displace the authority of England, attacked the authority of Shakespeare: Whitman saw the plays as dangerously anti-democratic and demanded that America discard them and 'see that it is, in itself, the final authority and reliance' (ibid., 283). Some writers showed how Shakespeare had penetrated American popular culture, as in Twain's use of *Hamlet* and *Macbeth* in *Huckleberry Finn* (1885), though Twain was never quite sure if Shakespeare was indeed the plays' author.

In many respects this variety of response was intriguingly similar to Russia where, after Mochalov's brilliant performance as Hamlet in 1837, *Hamlet* became as fashionable as throughout much of the rest of Europe, with young men priding themselves on their Hamletism in the wake of the popularity of Goethe's *Wilhelm Meister*. The 'superfluous man', introspective and self-regarding in his Hamlet-like pose, was attacked as useless egotism by Turgenev, especially in his story 'A Hamlet of Shchigrovsky District' (in *Sportsman's Sketches*, 1852) and his lecture on 'Hamlet and Don Quixote' (1860). It was an attack continued in Dostoevsky and in Chekhov but none was attacking Shakespeare; rather, the attack was on Russian intellectuals' misappropriation of Shakespeare. Through Shakespeare—and *Hamlet* in particular—different constructions of social responsibility and political engagement could be fought.

The attack on Shakespeare himself was mounted by Tolstoy in 1906 where the plays, especially *King Lear*, were indicted for poor dramaturgy, ineffective characterization, and, above all, an aristocratic disdain for the common people. Shakespeare is berated, in effect, for failing to be Tolstoy himself. Fanny Burney recorded George III complaining in 1785 'Was there ever . . . such stuff as a great part of Shakespeare? Only one must not say so!' (Gross, 113). But Tolstoy dared to say so: his are the most violent of all anti-Shakespearian diatribes, rejecting Shakespeare's drama as universally applicable and infinitely malleable.

Productions in Russia often played Shakespeare to audiences that made immediate political connections, necessitating interventions by censors: Shakespeare was banned in the Ukraine from 1863. Theatres across America, by contrast, often performed Shakespeare with a sense of national pride. The visit of Macready to New York in 1849 resulted in a riot and thirty-one deaths when working-class supporters of Edwin Forrest, the greatest American actor of his time, were encouraged to demonstrate their support for an American actor and against the English visitor and his wealthy American patrons. A number of English stars toured America including George Frederick Cooke and Edmund Kean. American Shakespeare actors toured England, James Hackett making a great success as Falstaff on both sides of the Atlantic for forty years, while the African-American Ira Aldridge starred as Macbeth, Shylock, and Richard III as well as Othello, playing in England and in Russia.

Shakespeare and the nineteenth-century English stage

In the interchange, America experienced all the changes in Shakespeare production being explored in England, as England also encountered European performers like Salvini who played Othello in Italian at Drury Lane in 1875 while the rest of the cast spoke English or Ernesto Rossi who played Hamlet, Lear, Macbeth, and Romeo there in 1876, also speaking Italian.

Charles Kemble produced *King John* in 1823 with a designer, James Robinson Planché, commissioned to search for and reproduce historical sources for the play's locations, costumes, and props. It was an extension of the research Charles Macklin undertook for his *Macbeth* in 1773 but it was at the centre of Victorian Shakespeare in the theatre. The plays, especially the tragedies and histories, became a resource for pictorial splendour with pageantry and stage spectacle, vast sets, and enormous casts of extras, aiming to create on stage the plays as historical narratives. Madame Vestris's ways with the comedies at Covent Garden in the 1840s showed that they too, especially *A Midsummer Night's Dream* (1840), could be spectacles of song and ballet. But elsewhere Shakespeare became the means by which history could be seen. As the centrepiece of English cultural history himself, he had become the sure guide to English and Roman history, now attested by the playbills' references to the British Museum as production resource. Attending a Shakespeare production—and especially looking at a Shakespeare production—was now an education in itself. Authenticity, not to Shakespeare and the conditions of early modern performance but to the historical reality to which it was a kind of window, was the key and the assumption continued through to the BBC television series of the plays (1978–85), where costuming had to be either early modern or of the historical date of the events Shakespeare dramatized.

Macready, concerned with raising the theatre's 'low' image, worked hard to redeem its ways with Shakespeare's texts. Restoring Shakespeare to the stage was one means of improving the theatre's cultural image. But he also prepared his productions more carefully than had been the norm, with frequent rehearsals (and long private work on his own performance) as well as thoughtful staging to manifest the historical accuracy of action and ritual as well as set and costumes. In England and America, which he toured three times, his work was highly praised and much imitated. Much hyped, Macready's restoration of the text was less substantial than his publicity promised: though his production of *King Lear* in 1838 restored Fool, after persuasion, and the tragic ending, never seen since Tate's version was first performed, Macready cut the blinding of Gloucester and his leap at Dover Cliff, the former presumably as too painful, the latter as dangerously close to comic. Macready's *King Lear* was set in an ancient Britain with signs of Stonehenge; his *Coriolanus* was in a modest Rome unlike the splendour of his *Julius Caesar*. But Macready also exploited the stage's technology for grand transformation scenes, for example in the images that backed the Chorus's speeches in his *Henry V*.

Charles Kean, the Eton-educated son of the dissolute Edmund, continued the trend in the 1850s at the Princess's Theatre. The productions became ever more populated, the interpolated scenes (for example Bolingbroke's arrival in London and Richard II's leaving it for prison) ever grander, the historical detail ever more obsessive. Kean was proud of being a fellow of the Society of Antiquaries and his published texts are full of annotation about historical accuracy—the same kind of detail that acted as commentary to Charles Knight's illustrated texts. The Chorus to *Henry V* became Clio, the Muse of History, and the images became *tableaux vivants* displayed behind a gauze, most famously for Henry's return to London. On stage crowds now numbered 200 or more, a visual representation of the nation (be it Rome or England), all exactly costumed, all demonstrating their historicity. The grand processions that had long been part of productions of, for instance, *Coriolanus* or *Henry VIII* were now inserted wherever space could be made. The effect is, in modern terms, operatic, the text subordinated to the visual. The English style of Shakespeare production influenced and in its turn was influenced by the work of the duke of Saxe-Meiningen's company, with its minutely disciplined crowds, seen in London in 1881.

Samuel Phelps's productions at Sadler's Wells from 1843 to 1862 made Shakespeare his house dramatist, producing thirty-two of the plays. More of Shakespeare's texts were restored but Phelps, while rarely swamping the play, made the diorama his speciality, allowing scenes to metamorphose into others and for characters to be seen journeying between the locations of scenes.

All serious productions were subject to intense scrutiny, not only in the increasingly important work of theatre reviewers who—like Hazlitt earlier, George Lewes in mid-century, and Bernard Shaw, Max Beerbohm, and Henry James at its end—minutely examined a production's adequacy to their individual views of the plays, but also in the mockery of their excesses in the steady stream of travesties.

While Henry Irving and Herbert Beerbohm Tree at the end of the century may have had successes with more plays and while their productions may have been even more spectacular, with Irving employing many fine painters to design his sets, and even more historically accurate, with Tree including the signing of Magna Carta, a scene Shakespeare inconveniently forgot to include in *King John*, there was little that changed the style of work that Macready, Phelps, and Charles Kean had defined. Grandeur dominated in acting as in design, relieved only rarely by the different virtues of domesticity, with extensive musical scores to accompany the action and long gaps while the huge sets were changed by armies of stagehands.

11

Modernist and multinational Shakespeare

New developments in theatre and scholarship

The opposition to these theatrical excesses came first from William Poel, who replaced one form of historical authenticity with another in his search to reproduce early modern theatrical conditions, complete with extras dressed as nobles to sit on stage as if members of the audience. His productions were much affected by the discovery of the De Witt drawing of the Swan Theatre: the first reliable depiction of an Elizabethan theatre interior. Mostly working with amateurs and in short runs in non-commercial spaces, Poel after 1881, when he produced *Hamlet* in first quarto guise, followed his lonely and much-mocked path. More traditionally and less eccentrically, Frank Benson's work, principally at the Shakespeare Memorial Theatre from 1886 to 1919, showed how modest ambition in the service of the text could make Shakespeare both popular and pleasurable.

Edward Gordon Craig, son of Ellen Terry, moved in his theory and practice to a different resistance to the principles of high Victorian spectacular theatre. He explored both abstraction and simplicity, culminating in the use of moveable screens to define space for his *Hamlet*, codirected with Stanislavsky at the Moscow Art Theatre in 1912. Craig's project was explicitly modernist in its assumptions and as startling when underpinning Sally Jacobs's set for Peter Brook's *A Midsummer Night's Dream* (Royal Shakespeare Company, 1970) as when Craig created a church out of light alone for *Much Ado about Nothing* in 1903.

Most influential of all was Harley Granville-Barker, who briefly worked with Poel. His productions of *The Winter's Tale*, *Twelfth Night*, and *A Midsummer Night's Dream* (with a man as Oberon, fairies with gold-leafed faces, and folk tunes as music) at the Savoy (1912–14) revolutionized production technique. But far more influential were his *Prefaces to Shakespeare*, the first of which appeared in 1923. In their mixture of the scholarly and the practical, combining theatrical awareness with close attention to Shakespeare's dramatic technique, they made directors aware of the virtues of the text and students and scholars aware of the plays as dramas. They marked a new meeting of theatre and scholarship in Shakespeare studies.

The *Prefaces* were designed for the mythical general reader but Shakespeare studies were increasingly professional and visibly a growth industry. The archival and bibliographical work of Victorian scholars such as James Orchard Halliwell-Phillipps and John Payne Collier, for all the latter's forgeries of documents that might help his arguments (and which continue to confuse scholars), led to further biographical and contextual study. Sidney Lee's work on the many figures surrounding Shakespeare for the *Dictionary of National Biography* helped his much-reprinted and expanded biography (first published in 1898), based on his dictionary entry. The work of Charles William Wallace (1865–1932) and his wife at the Public

Record Office added crucial new fragments of knowledge about Shakespeare's life to offset the continuing strain of biographical speculations by, for instance, Oscar Wilde in his fictional *A Portrait of Mr W. H.* (1889) or Frank Harris in his supposedly non-fictional *The Man Shakespeare* (1909).

But there was also a new kind of biographical enquiry, working from the plays to construct a version of Shakespeare's mind. Edward Dowden's *Shakspere: a Critical Study of his Mind and Art* (1875) saw the plays as veiled emotional and intellectual autobiography. Caroline Spurgeon's investigation in *Shakespeare's Imagery and What it Tells Us* (1935) enumerated patterns of images to reveal Shakespeare's own likes and dislikes.

In the first half of the twentieth century the theatrical research of Sir E. K. Chambers and G. E. Bentley and the bibliographical work of Sir W. W. Greg became cornerstones of highly accomplished academic study, often building on the achievements of Germanic classical and Shakespearian scholarship. For Chambers it led towards distinguished work on Shakespeare's biography. The image-centred criticism of Caroline Spurgeon and the historical contextual work of E. M. W. Tillyard, Wilson Knight's thematic criticism and the interest in the history of ideas by Hardin Craig and Theodore Spencer, the growth of the close reading in New Criticism and the work of William Empson, all began major modes of critical interpretative approaches to Shakespeare which profoundly affected the ways the plays were read and taught.

There were new and major series of editions, building on the earlier accomplishments of Edmond Malone and hardly changing the premises of such editing: the American-based

 New Variorum begun by H. H. Furness in 1871 and continued by his son (and still ongoing); the Arden Shakespeare started with *Hamlet*, edited by Edward Dowden, in 1899 and is now in its third complete series; the New Shakespeare, published by Cambridge University Press (1921–66), was edited by Sir Arthur Quiller-Couch and John Dover Wilson, who was responsible for both its most incisive scholarship and some comically excessive invented stage directions.

Critical interpretations could become best-sellers. In A. C. Bradley's *Shakespearean Tragedy* (1904), for example, though the plays are treated more like novels or biographies of great men, a new orthodoxy of critical reading was defined. Guy Boas argued wittily in 1926:

> I dreamt last night that Shakespeare's ghost
> Sat for a Civil Service post;
> The English paper for the year
> Had several questions on *King Lear*
> Which Shakespeare answered very badly
> Because he hadn't read his Bradley.
> (Gross, 329)

Shakespeare and the British empire

Shakespeare, as a cornerstone of Englishness, was part of many kinds of official examination for future administrators of the empire and his work was vigorously championed by, for instance, the British Empire Shakespeare Society, founded in 1901 to encourage reading circles and costume recitals. In 1912 the 'Shakespeare's England' exhibition at Earl's Court in London, complete with the first-ever replica of the Globe Theatre, celebrated Shakespeare as heritage culture in a display of stirring nationalism.

The events in 1916 for the tercentenary of Shakespeare's death, an event marked almost as strongly in Germany as in England, included publication of a major collection of essays on Shakespeare's times, *Shakespeare's England*, as well as a Shakespeare day for schools (complete with a Shakespeare prayer) and, as a sign of Shakespeare's international importance, *A Book of Homage to Shakespeare* edited by Israel Gollancz as secretary of the tercentenary committee, with a poem by Thomas Hardy and with contributions from all corners of the empire carefully placed before those from the rest of the world. Many years later the British Council, as an offshoot of government charged with promoting British culture worldwide, sponsored the Marlowe Society's complete audio recordings of the plays, directed by George Rylands (1958–64), records that functioned as 'official' Shakespeare across the world.

The countries of the empire often developed complexly ambivalent attitudes towards Shakespeare, seeing him both as the embodiment of their colonial masters and as something enticingly able to be appropriated into other forms, ready to be made a part of indigenous dramatic traditions. In India, for instance, Shakespeare was being performed in Calcutta from the 1780s and in Bombay in the 1850s. There were popular adaptations of Shakespeare's plots into Marathi, Gujarati, and Parsi, each culture finding rich resources for its own styles of popular theatre. Aga Hashr Kashmiri, who adapted many Shakespeare plays into Urdu in the late nineteenth and early twentieth centuries, acquired the nickname 'Shakespeare-e-Hind' ('Shakespeare of India'). Indian rulers often commanded private performances of the plays, for example *Cymbeline* performed at the wedding of the maharaja of Baroda in 1879.

 English companies toured India (like, later, Geoffrey Kendal's troupe, filmed as *Shakespeare Wallah* in 1965) and the English residents of the raj put on amateur productions. Schools, educating Indian students in the high cultural forms that the proponents of empire thought would raise them to European standards, staged Shakespeare performances as English schools so regularly did. The opposition was replicated throughout the empire: on the one hand, imitations, often amateur or second-rate, of English styles of Shakespeare production; on the other, energized and vital re-imaginations of Shakespeare into other, local, modes of theatre.

Colonial and post-colonial responses to Shakespeare, however, often rewrote Shakespeare as a means of reconsidering the relationship of nation to empire. *The Tempest*, often seen as a narrative of colonialism, became in Octave Mannoni's *Psychology of Colonisation* (1950) the epitome of the process as 'Prospero complex' faced 'Caliban complex'. For many Caribbean writers, like the Barbadian George Lamming in the autobiographical *The Pleasures of Exile* (1960) and the novel *Water with Berries* (1971), Aimé Césaire (from Martinique) in his play *Une tempête* (1968), Edward Brathwaite (from Barbados) in his poem 'Caliban' in *Islands* (1969), and the Cuban Roberto Retamar in 'Caliban' (1974), exploring the play is the way for them, seeing themselves as Calibans, to identify their own political positioning.

Crossing national boundaries

In this these writers were hardly unusual. Across the world in the twentieth century, whether in parts of the (former) British empire or not, writers found in Shakespeare as potent a way of voicing themselves as had earlier generations, and states found Shakespeare co-opted in opposition to their political oppressions. Throughout the Soviet bloc, for instance, Shakespeare was censored as dangerously subversive, controlled into a political acceptability as an example of socialist realism, or banned, as *Hamlet* was under Stalin. Some plays began to be admired because praised by Marx (for example, *Timon of Athens*) or Engels (for example, *The Merry Wives of Windsor*). But writers opposing Sovietism like Blok, Akhmatova, Tsvetaeva, and Pasternak turned to Shakespeare, the last both translating *Hamlet* and *King Lear* (used for Grigory Kozintsev's film versions in 1964 and 1971) and making *Hamlet* the basis of poems in his banned novel *Doctor Zhivago* (1958).

Elsewhere, in less oppressive contexts, Shakespeare was being rethought and remade. In Japan, for instance, *The Merchant of Venice* was played in a Kabuki adaptation in 1885 while the first Japanese translation (*Julius Caesar* by Shoyo Tsubouchi) appeared a few years later. Later translations were crucial in the development of Shingeki, the new theatre that explored modern forms of realism within a Japanese context. Novels and short stories derived from Shakespearian materials were written throughout the century. But perhaps the most visible signs of Japanese Shakespeare have been the films of Akira Kurosawa: *Castle of the Spider's Web* (from *Macbeth*, also known as *Throne of Blood*, 1957), *The Bad Sleep Well* (from *Hamlet*, 1960), and *Ran* (*Chaos*, from *King Lear*, 1985); and the theatre productions of Yukio Ninagawa, especially his *Macbeth* (1980), *The Tempest* (1987), and *A Midsummer Night's Dream* (1994). Where Kurosawa rethought Shakespeare's narratives into Japanese history without using a line of Shakespeare's, Ninagawa used a range of Japanese theatrical styles and cultural concepts to contextualize the plays.

However one looks at it, Shakespeare had become a global phenomenon. There were translations of his plays and poems into a vast array of languages, including Swedish (1813), Greek (1855), Hebrew (1874), Welsh (1874), Dutch (1880), Bulgarian (1881), Yiddish (1886), Arabic (1890s), Korean (1906), Scottish Gaelic (1911), Chinese (1922), and Maori (2000). Academics, teachers, and enthusiasts formed Shakespeare societies to rival the German one in, for example, the USA (1923, refounded 1973), Japan (1962), Korea (1963), France (1977), Australia and New Zealand (1990), the Low Countries (1993), and even Britain (2002). The International Shakespeare Association was created in 1974. A touring exhibition of materials from the Folger Shakespeare Library (1979–81) was justly called 'Shakespeare: the Globe and the World'.

12 Worldwide Will

Shakespeare and film

Shakespeare's global presence had been altered irrevocably by the development of film. His plays started to be recorded almost as soon as sound recordings began; performances were no longer to be contained within the theatre. Edwin Booth had been recorded in 1890 with a speech from *Othello* and Ellen Terry, Henry Irving, and Beerbohm Tree were also caught on cylinder. *Hamlet* was sold 'complete' on ten 78 r.p.m. discs with John Gielgud, *Macbeth* in Orson Welles's Mercury Theatre production. But the technologies of the LP made full-length recordings more practicable. Great actors—and many not-so-great—could be heard in schools and at home, making the sound of Shakespeare spoken part of the educational and domestic experience of Shakespeare. He entered the home too as part of radio, especially from the BBC which started broadcasting Shakespeare in 1923 and for which Shakespeare has been the backbone of the radio drama repertory ever since. Hundreds of radio productions of the plays have been mounted, often with distinguished casts: Donald Wolfit, John Gielgud, Michael Redgrave, and Alec Guinness have all played Lear on radio. Radio has also generated vast numbers of critical, biographical, and theatrical features on Shakespeare, a significant part of the way that both Shakespeare's life and his work have been thought about.

If Shakespeare on audio disc is necessarily invisible Shakespeare, the first films were necessarily silent Shakespeare. The earliest fragment to survive is the death of King John in Beerbohm Tree's production, filmed in 1899, though how much more was filmed is unclear. The film company, Biograph, was bidding for respectability, and Shakespeare was its route towards it. Sarah Bernhardt was filmed duelling as Hamlet in 1900 and there were further extracts from Georges Méliès in 1907. In the following years there were hundreds of silent Shakespeares, most short, some an hour or more in length—for example, a 1912 American *Richard III* with Frederick Warde and the 1913 *Hamlet* with Sir Johnston Forbes-Robertson.

If initially their style of film acting was overtly theatrical (and in Warde's case could be contrasted with readings and lectures by him 'live' in the gaps between reels at screenings), the film techniques were rapidly becoming sophisticated, encouraging a number of versions of Shakespeare's supernatural plays, *A Midsummer Night's Dream* and *The Tempest*, which could make good use of trick effects. In 1916 Tree was lured to America to film *Macbeth* but was mocked by the British press for succumbing to such commercialism. By the 1920s there were unquestionably major accomplishments in filmed Shakespeare, especially from Germany with Svend Gade's 1920 adaptation of *Hamlet* (with Asta Nielsen as a female prince) and Buchowetski's 1922 *Othello* with Emil Jannings. There were also silent Shakespeare documentaries, fiction films with Shakespeare as a character, and Shakespeare parodies. Most strikingly, silent film was a genuinely international product (and it is significant how many of the films came from Italy and Germany and how few from England), for the intertitles could be easily remade into any language.

There have been fewer Shakespeare sound films in the more than seventy years of the talkies than silent films in the previous thirty. Most of the silents are lost. Many of the sound films are widely available on video and DVD and have become a major element in teaching Shakespeare at school and university. In cinemas and homes, as well as schools, Shakespeare on film is by far the most common experience of Shakespeare in performance. Sound film has formed the modern popular images of performed Shakespeare, a sequence culminating in the success of Shakespeare himself on film in *Shakespeare in Love* (1998), which won seven Oscars with its image of Shakespeare as young romantic genius in search of his muse, the inverse of the Droeshout engraving.

Hollywood quickly recognized the possibilities of Shakespeare for talking pictures. *The Taming of the Shrew* with Mary Pickford and Douglas Fairbanks (1929) was at the bridge between silents and sound, but Warner Brothers' spectacular *A Midsummer Night's Dream* (1935), based on Max Reinhardt's production and with a host of stars, great spectacle, much of Mendelssohn's music, and less than half of Shakespeare's words, showed what could be done. It was not, however, financially successful.

Laurence Olivier, who had played Orlando in a Hollywood *As You Like It* (1936), saw the possibilities for a heroic celebration of England in the middle of the Second World War in making *Henry V* as a form of patriotic epic, starting from a nostalgic vision of the unblitzed London before a performance at the

 Globe. His broodingly Oedipal *Hamlet* (1948) and comically villainous *Richard III* (1955), another version of Shakespeare as guide to English history, defined English Shakespeare films as safe and traditional. The same was true of the rare American forays (for example, *Julius Caesar* in 1953 and 1970), star-studded epics echoing Hollywood's Roman epics.

Far more brilliantly, Orson Welles, with radical rethinking of the possibilities of cinema and meagre budgets, made incisive and complex versions of *Macbeth* (1948), *Othello* (1952), and the *Henry IV* plays as *Chimes at Midnight* (1966). If the 1960s were dominated by Franco Zeffirelli's popular and lush *The Taming of the Shrew* (1966) and *Romeo and Juliet* (1968), there were powerfully intelligent and superbly cinematic alternatives in Kurosawa's Japanese re-imaginings and Grigory Kozintsev's political readings of *Hamlet* (1964) and *King Lear* (1970), with great performances from Innokenti Smoktunovski as Hamlet and Yuri Yarvets as Lear and the benefits of Shostakovich's fine film-scores.

While there were a number of films that did little more—and often rather less—than record successful stage productions, capturing a shadow of, for example, Olivier's performance as Othello (1965), a new era for popular and commercially successful Shakespeare films began with Kenneth Branagh's *Henry V* (1989). Branagh followed it with *Much Ado about Nothing* (1993) and a full-text, four-hour *Hamlet* (1996). Baz Luhrmann's *William Shakespeare's Romeo + Juliet* (1996) exploited the resources of film as never before, as well as using stars popular with teenage audiences, while Ian McKellen transformed his stage performance of Richard III into a narrative of an alternative twentieth-century history (directed by Richard Loncraine, 1996).

Some of the most thoughtful and experimental work in filming Shakespeare has come from Britain, including Peter Brook's *King Lear* (with Paul Scofield, 1971), Derek Jarman's *The Tempest* (1979), Peter Greenaway's *Prospero's Books* (1991, from *The Tempest*, with John Gielgud playing all the roles), and Christine Edzard's *As You Like It* (1992). But Shakespeare has also been a major source for films that are offshoots, using a Shakespeare play as the underpinning for their own plots, for example *Forbidden Planet* (1956, from *The Tempest*), *Men of Respect* (1990, from *Macbeth*), and *The Lion King* (1994, from *Hamlet*).

Shakespeare and twentieth-century literature

Throughout the twentieth century novelists and playwrights continued to work with and from Shakespeare to create their own dramas. The range has been immense and a very few examples in little more than a list must stand for all. *The Tempest* stands behind John Fowles's *The Magus* (1966) and Iris Murdoch's *The Sea, the Sea* (1978) as well as Toni Morrison's *Tar Baby* (1981) and Gloria Naylor's *Mama Day* (1988). Jane Smiley re-imagined *King Lear* in the American mid-west in *A Thousand Acres* (1991), while Robert Nye gave an extradramatic life to *Falstaff* (1976) and to *Mrs Shakespeare* (1993). *Hamlet* lies within Virginia Woolf's *Between the Acts* (1941), John Updike's *Gertrude and Claudius* (1999), and many murder mysteries, though the Shakespeare variety reached its apogee in James Thurber's 'The Macbeth murder mystery'. There have also been serious fictional biographies of Shakespeare, for example, Anthony Burgess's *Nothing Like the Sun* (1964), and a superb comic one, Caryl Brahms's and S. J. Simon's *No Bed for Bacon* (1941).

On the stage Shakespeare has become a basis for musicals: for example, *The Boys from Syracuse* (1938, from *The Comedy of Errors*, music by Richard Rodgers), *Kiss Me Kate* (1948, from *The Taming of the Shrew*, music by Cole Porter), and *West Side Story* (1957, from *Romeo and Juliet*, music by Leonard Bernstein). There have been sequels and prequels (for example, Howard Barker's *Seven Lears*, 1990, and Elaine Feinstein's and the Women's Theatre Group's *Lear's Daughters*, 1991), plays developing minor characters (Tom Stoppard's *Rosencrantz and Guildenstern are Dead*, 1966) and rethinking the action (Edward Bond's *Lear*, 1971, Eugène Ionesco's *Macbett*, 1972, Charles Marowitz's collage versions collected as *The Marowitz Shakespeare*, 1978), plays providing cultural relocations (Welcome Msomi's *uMabatha*, 1972) and political reinterpretations (for example, Bertolt Brecht's *Coriolanus*, 1964, or his use of *Richard III* in *The Life of Galileo*, 1943, and *The Resistible Rise of Arturo Ui*, 1957). There have also been major successes in relocating plays to the opera house, especially Benjamin Britten's *A Midsummer Night's Dream* (1960), Samuel Barber's *Antony and Cleopatra* (1966), and Aribert Reimann's *Lear* (1978), and one superb translation to ballet in the successive choreographic interpretations of Prokofiev's *Romeo and Juliet* (1935) by Ashton, Cranko, MacMillan, and others.

Shakespeare on the twentieth-century stage

But as well as these adaptations for the stage, the plays themselves have a long and complex history of twentieth-century stage performance. Productions in continental Europe were often thoughtfully political and strikingly modernist in design, for example Leopold Jessner's *Richard III* (1920) and *Othello* (1921), both in Berlin, or the versions of *Julius Caesar* by Leon Schiller (Warsaw, 1928) and Jirí Frejka (Prague, 1936). Such work was echoed by Orson Welles's stage work in America, with his 'voodoo' *Macbeth* and his strongly anti-fascist *Julius Caesar* in 1937.

But little similar was seen in England, with the notable exception of Terence Gray's *Richard III* (Cambridge, 1928) and Theodore Komisarjevsky's productions at Stratford (for example, *King Lear*, 1936). British experiment was more often more restrained: Barry Jackson startled London when his 1925 modern-dress *Hamlet* had Hamlet in plus fours, but there was nothing radical about Jackson's reading of the play. Lilian Baylis's commitment to Shakespeare at the Old Vic Theatre led to all the plays in the first folio being produced there under Robert Atkins, ending in 1923 with *Troilus and Cressida*, a play whose stage history effectively began in the twentieth century. In the aftermath of his triumphant performances as Richard II (1929) and Hamlet (1930), John Gielgud turned to directing: his *Romeo and Juliet* (1935) at the New Theatre, with Laurence Olivier exchanging Mercutio for Romeo during the run, was most remarkable for the sets by the three women designers known as Motley, whose abstracted forms allowed for fluid staging. Their designs transformed Shakespeare productions from Victorian ponderousness to a new light rapidity.

In Stratford the Shakespeare Memorial Theatre reopened in 1932 after a fire in 1926. Its productions, often dull, occasionally brilliant, changed when Peter Brook arrived to direct *Love's Labour's Lost* in 1946 and *Titus Andronicus* in 1955, two previously unfashionable plays whose stageworthiness was newly proven. In 1960 Peter Hall created the Royal Shakespeare Company (RSC), with a permanent ensemble company and year-round work in Stratford and London. Brook's Beckett-influenced *King Lear* (1962), a production developed from an essay by the Polish Shakespeare critic Jan Kott, and Hall's *The Wars of the Roses* (with John Barton, 1963–4) were early indications that the RSC could create powerful and innovative work to rival the best by European directors as well as their sustained advocacy of plays previously unfashionable, especially *Troilus and Cressida* and *Measure for Measure*. Buzz Goodbody's creation of The Other Place, a small studio-theatre in Stratford, defined radical new ways for the RSC to play Shakespeare in small spaces (for example, her *Hamlet* in 1975 and Trevor Nunn's *Macbeth* in 1976).

In North America the post-war period was most marked by the rapid growth of theatres hosting Shakespeare festivals, like Tyrone Guthrie's at Stratford, Ontario, from 1953 or Joseph Papp's New York Shakespeare Festival in Central Park from 1954 or at Ashland, Oregon. By the end of the century there were seventy Shakespeare festivals across the continent. In western Europe directors, many heavily influenced by Brechtian principles, searched the plays for political meanings, most excitingly in the work of Roger Planchon in France and Giorgio Strehler in Italy (especially *The Tempest* in 1978). In the Soviet bloc after 1968 officially acceptable productions had to compete with productions that used Shakespeare to encode criticism of the state, for example Yuri Lyubimov's *Hamlet* (Moscow, 1971).

In the last quarter of the century English Shakespeare production outside the still-flourishing RSC (under Peter Hall, Trevor Nunn, Terry Hands, Adrian Noble, and Michael Boyd) and the fine work at the Royal National Theatre varied from the excellent traditional work at the Regent's Park Open Air Theatre in London to the popular and political productions of Michael Bogdanov's and Michael Pennington's English

Shakespeare Company (*The Wars of the Roses*, 1987–8) to the defiant northern voices of Barrie Rutter's Northern Broadsides (from 1992). In London a long campaign to build an authentic reconstruction of the Globe, an often uneasy collaboration between Sam Wanamaker's single-minded drive, architects, and scholars, resulted finally in Shakespeare's Globe opening in 1997 and playing thereafter to large and appreciative audiences. If the economics of theatre made Shakespeare's large casts problematic, there were innovative solutions in every corner of the country.

For the first time a significant number of women directed Shakespeare, including Ariane Mnouchkine in France, Karin Beier in Germany, and Deborah Warner and Jude Kelly in England. Productions experimented with cross-cultural influences, especially after the success in the West of Ninagawa's work. Productions could be played with cross-gendered casting, with multilingual casts, with barely a shred of Shakespeare's text, or without a line being cut. Productions could last one hour or six, with casts of fifty or two, with massive sets or none, in daylight or with complex lighting, in theatres large and small or in the street. In Britain, in particular, Shakespeare is also the staple of amateur production with many thousands of performances every year by schoolchildren of all ages, by university societies, and by local groups brand-new and long-established. Shakespeare seems still to be everywhere where theatre is being made: in China in 1986 a Shakespeare festival gathered twenty-eight Chinese productions; in the 1990s there were over forty productions of *Hamlet* in Korea. Always provoking theatre workers and stretching them to their limits, Shakespeare is unquestionably still the major driving force in world theatre.

13 The universal author

Shakespeare and education

In many of the world's educational systems Shakespeare remains at the core of literary study, compulsory in the English national curriculum at secondary school and all but compulsory in many other countries. At universities his plays are central to the study of literature and drama and, though political battles in the United States to revise the canon of literary study led to Shakespeare no longer being compulsory at many universities, more students than ever take Shakespeare courses there. The editing of Shakespeare has responded to these different needs with innovative editions for schools (for example, Rex Gibson's Cambridge School Shakespeare, from 1991), major student editions of the complete works (for example, edited by Peter Alexander, 1951; the Riverside Shakespeare, 1974, 2nd edn 1997; and the Norton Shakespeare, 1997), and repeated revisions of established series or forms of presentation (for example, the New Cambridge, Oxford, and Arden Third series).

Shakespeare editing has been transformed by new principles of textual bibliography but also by the availability of computers, on-line databases and web-delivered editions. New theories about the early texts, especially that they represent for some plays (for example, *King Lear*) successive stages of Shakespeare's own revision of the plays, have led to the appearance of multiple-text editions, in the wake of the inclusion of both quarto- and folio-derived texts of *Lear* in the Oxford Shakespeare, edited by Stanley Wells and Gary Taylor (1986). Successive movements in scholarship have produced dramatic changes in the understanding of Shakespeare's sources, the printing of the folio, Shakespeare's processes of composition, and the cultural, political, and theatrical contexts within which he wrote.

The development of major resources for scholars has included the Folger Shakespeare Library, opened in 1932 with the collection of Henry Clay Folger and amounting to the world's largest collection of Shakespeare materials, with seventy-nine copies of the first folio; the Shakespeare Centre Library in Stratford upon Avon, which includes the RSC's archives; and the Shakespeare Institute of the University of Birmingham, founded by Allardyce Nicoll in 1951. Shakespeare conferences proliferate, but the annual conference of the Shakespeare Association of America, the biennial International Shakespeare Conference in Stratford upon Avon, and the quinquennial World Shakespeare Congress each gather many hundreds of scholars from all over the world. There are numerous Shakespeare journals, including *Shakespeare Survey* (started by Nicoll in 1948), *Shakespeare Newsletter* (from 1951), two called *Shakespeare Studies* (in Japan from 1961 and the USA since 1965), and, from 1950, the Folger-based *Shakespeare Quarterly*, whose annual listing of publications in its World Shakespeare Bibliography (now available online) testifies to the colossal output of the academic Shakespeare industry.

There are times when the multiple modes of Shakespeare criticism can seem bewildering—with, in the last quarter of the twentieth century, such dominant strands as new historicism, cultural materialism, feminist studies and gender criticism, queer theory, and cultural studies. Psychoanalytical approaches seem to have little connection with stage- and film-oriented ones. The study of the material culture of early modern England seems to be radically distinct as a mode of academic investigation from the history of Shakespeare translation. The exploration of Renaissance reading habits can seem to sit uncomfortably beside studies in Shakespeare pedagogy.

Not the least important part of this activity has been biographical study. There have been so many biographies of Shakespeare that Samuel Schoenbaum wrote a large as well as entertaining study of the history of Shakespeare biography, *Shakespeare's Lives* (1970). Among the most important biographies of recent years have been Schoenbaum's *William Shakespeare: a Documentary Life* (1975), Park Honan's *Shakespeare: a Life* (1998), Katherine Duncan-Jones's *Ungentle Shakespeare* (2001), and James Shapiro's *1599: A Year in the Life of William Shakespeare* (2005)—each contributing significantly to our understanding of the facts and the interpretation of the hypotheses concerning Shakespeare's life.

But the plurality of Shakespeare studies is united by the extraordinary range of meanings provoked by Shakespeare. As much concerned with the history of Shakespeare's afterlife as with close analysis of particular texts, as interested in Shakespeare in twenty-first-century Brazil as in sixteenth-century London, as excited by Shakespeare in nineteenth-century Hebrew as in early modern English, Shakespeare studies engage with every aspect of the culture that produced Shakespeare and the cultures his work has produced.

For if Shakespeare has often seemed to some to be the prerogative of English high culture, then throughout the world Shakespeare, his image, and his works have been appropriated for every kind of popular cultural usage, signs both of his cultural authority and of the cultural contestation his works provoke.

In Britain politicians of the left and right rely on Shakespeare as a national and quasi-religious authority for their political creeds. The Labour leader Neil Kinnock, the heir to nineteenth-century political oratory with its predilection for quoting Shakespeare, required his speech-writers to know the Bible and Shakespeare, the twin bedrocks of working-class culture. At the opposite end of the political spectrum, right-wing Conservative politicians like Michael Portillo returned with mechanical frequency to Ulysses's speech on degree in *Troilus and Cressida* as 'proof' that Shakespeare supported the hierarchies and institutions tories were committed to maintain.

Shakespeare's plays are quoted in every kind of popular film and television programme. Episodes in many situation comedies show how contested the place of Shakespeare is in American or British society as children wrestle with Shakespeare homework, parents quote Shakespeare defiantly, or the school Shakespeare production looms. The last of the original *Star Trek* films, *Star Trek VI* (1991), quotes Shakespeare in its subtitle, *The Undiscovered Country*, and jokes about Shakespeare sounding better in the original Klingon, a language invented for the television series whose devotees have indeed 'translated' *Hamlet* into Klingon (2000). There are pornographic films with fragments of Shakespearian plots (both heterosexual and homosexual) and strip clubs that have tried to avoid censorship by having the strippers speak Shakespeare's lines.

In the camp horror film *Theatre of Blood* (1973), a disgruntled Shakespearian actor, played by Vincent Price, murders theatre critics in appropriately Shakespearian ways. The science-fiction film *Forbidden Planet* (1956) spawned a musical stage adaptation, *Return to the Forbidden Planet* (1989), which used classic rock songs and Shakespearian puns ('Beware the Ids that march'). Versions of twelve plays, made as animated 30-minute episodes by S4C, a Welsh television company, in collaboration with Russian animators, were screened in 1992, the texts adapted by Leon Garfield, author of short narrative versions for children, successors to Lambs' *Tales*.

There are strip cartoons which use the entire Shakespeare text in speech bubbles as well as one which shows Shakespeare being given his plots by supernatural beings. A British heavyweight boxer, Frank Bruno, appeared on television in drag in a comedy sketch in which he played Juliet in the balcony scene. Shakespeare's lines appear in rock songs and rap, while a serious popular singer Elvis Costello collaborated with the classical Brodsky Quartet on *The Juliet Letters* (1996), whose lyrics are imaginary letters to Shakespeare's heroine. When listeners to BBC Radio 4's *Today* programme voted Shakespeare the 'Man of the millennium' in 1999, there was hardly any surprise at the choice. Castaways on *Desert Island Discs* on BBC, the world's longest-running radio programme, are always allowed a copy of Shakespeare as well as the Bible for their island.

Shakespeare and his characters have been extensively used for advertising. There are cigars named Hamlet, Romeo y Julieta, Falstaff, and Antonio y Cleopatra. His own image and his characters have been used to sell, for example, Ford cars, Shell petrol, Schweppes soft drinks, and Maxwell House coffee and, since 1986, Coca-Cola, Shreddies breakfast cereal, Typhoo tea, and Carling Black Label lager.

Shakespeare has appeared on English banknotes, as a hologram on British cheque-guarantee cards, and on playing cards. His characters have made up chess sets and cigarette cards. There are statues, streets, squares, piazzas, and avenues named after Shakespeare and after his most famous characters in many cities of the world. There are Shakespeare pubs in many British airports and an American company, Celebriducks, sells plastic Shakespeare ducks for the bath. Souvenirs from Stratford have been available since the eighteenth century and ceramic images of Shakespeare as figurines, on plates, toby jugs, and on the tops of walking-sticks proliferated in the nineteenth.

More seriously, the Shakespeare tourist industry is a vital component of the economic stability of the West Midlands region in England and theatre companies like the Royal Shakespeare Company and Shakespeare's Globe are major employers. There are no figures available for the value of the global Shakespeare economy, but it must run to many billions of pounds per annum. Quite what this extraordinary plethora of Shakespeare material means lies outside the scope of this account. Its mere existence testifies eloquently to the overwhelming presence of Shakespeare, both the man and his works, throughout almost every aspect of the world's culture, in almost every language, in ways often so familiar as hardly to be noticed. His biography, the history of his life and his cultural afterlives, is not only national but triumphantly international.

Sources

R. Bearman, *Shakespeare in the Stratford records* (1994) · E. K. Chambers, *William Shakespeare: a study of facts and problems*, 2 vols. (1930) · K. Duncan-Jones, *Ungentle Shakespeare* (2001) · M. Eccles, *Shakespeare in Warwickshire* (1961) · P. Honan, *Shakespeare: a life* (1998) · E. A. J. Honigmann, *Shakespeare: the 'lost' years*, 2nd edn (1998) · S. Schoenbaum, *William Shakespeare: a documentary life* (1975) · S. Schoenbaum, *William Shakespeare: records and images* (1981) · S. Schoenbaum, *William Shakespeare: a compact documentary life*, rev. edn (1987) · P. Thomson, *Shakespeare's professional career* (1992) · S. Wells, *Shakespeare: a dramatic life* (1994) · *William Shakespeare: the complete works*, ed. S. Wells and G. Taylor (1986) · S. Wells and G. Taylor, *William Shakespeare: a textual companion* (1987) · M. Wiggins, *Shakespeare and the drama of his time* (2000) · J. Bate, *Shakespeare and the English Romantic imagination* (1986) · J. Bate, *Shakespearean constitutions* (1989) · J. Bate, *The genius of Shakespeare* (1997) · J. Bate, ed., *The Romantics on Shakespeare* (1992) · J. Bate and R. Jackson, eds., *Shakespeare: an illustrated stage history* (1996) · M. de Grazia and S. Wells, *The Cambridge companion to Shakespeare* (2001) · M. Dobson, *The making of the national poet* (1992) · M. Dobson and S. Wells, *The Oxford companion to Shakespeare* (2001) · J. Gross, *After Shakespeare* (2002) · W. Hortmann, *Shakespeare on the German stage: the twentieth century* (1998) · R. Jackson, ed., *The Cambridge companion to Shakespeare on film* (2000) · D. Scott Kastan, *A companion to Shakespeare* (1999) · D. Kennedy, *Looking at Shakespeare*,

2nd edn (2001) · D. Kennedy, ed., *Foreign Shakespeare* (1993) · D. Lanier, *Shakespeare and modern popular culture* (2002) · A. Loomba and M. Orkin, *Post-colonial Shakespeares* (1998) · P. Rawlings, ed., *Americans on Shakespeare, 1776–1914* (1999) · *The works of William Shakespear*, ed. N. Rowe, 6 vols. (1709) · T. Sasayama and others, eds., *Shakespeare and the Japanese stage* (1998) · G. Taylor, *Reinventing Shakespeare* (1989) · A. Thompson and S. Roberts, eds., *Women reading Shakespeare, 1660–1900* (1997) · B. Vickers, ed., *Shakespeare: the critical heritage, 1623–1801*, 6 vols. (1974–81) · S. Wells and S. Stanton, *The Cambridge companion to Shakespeare on stage* (2002) · S. Williams, *Shakespeare on the German stage, 1586–1914* (1990)

Index

S